ANGLO-SAXON ART

1 The Fuller Brooch.
Silver inlaid with niello. The human figures represent
the five senses – sight, taste, smell, hearing and touch.
Diameter 11.4 cm. (London, British Museum)

DAVID M. WILSON

ANGLO-SAXON ART

FROM THE SEVENTH CENTURY TO
THE NORMAN CONQUEST

The Overlook Press
Woodstock, New York

First published in the United States by
The Overlook Press
Lewis Hollow Road
Woodstock, New York 12498
Text copyright © 1984 David M. Wilson
Illustrations and layout copyright © 1984 Thames and Hudson Ltd

Library of Congress Cataloging in Publication Data

Wilson, David Mackenzie.
   Anglo-Saxon art.

   Includes index.
   1. Art, Anglo-Saxon.   I. Title.
N6763.W55   1984   709'.42   84-4447
ISBN 0-87951-976-2

Printed in Japan

CONTENTS

To Eva

Preface

AN ACADEMIC ADMINISTRATOR has little opportunity for original research, but the itch to work within his subject is always present. This book helps to relieve such an itch, but it has a serious purpose in that it is more than thirty years since one of my predecessors, Sir Thomas Kendrick, completed a two-volume survey of Anglo-Saxon art which is still the main work of synthesis on the subject. In this book I present a view of Anglo-Saxon art in the light of the many new finds and theories which have been introduced since Tom Kendrick wrote. In any book of synthesis much detail has to be omitted, many statements elided: I am aware that the omissions will not please everybody and that some will treat my elisions with contumely, but I hope that I have provided for the layman and student alike an introduction to the present state of study of the most brilliant period of Anglo-Saxon art.

I have throughout used the county names as they existed before the boundary revisions of April 1974.

I am indebted to many scholars who have helped me in answering queries; to many museum curators and clergymen who have allowed me to see, touch and discuss objects in their care; and to many friends and acquaintances in this country and abroad who have answered casual queries with elegance and patience. I am grateful to a number of illustrators and photographers to whom detailed acknowledgment is made elsewhere: but I should particularly thank Tony Milton, who has produced new colour images of British Museum material of the highest standard under conditions of some stress; and, as always, my wife, who has not only put up with abolished week-ends but has also drawn many of the figures.

I must thank a number of scholars for particular help. Milly Budny for conversation about manuscripts and Rosemary Cramp for help with sculpture; but particularly Leslie Webster and James Graham-Campbell for reading an early draft of this book with commendable speed and patient criticism (most of which I have accepted with alacrity). Lastly to Marjorie Caygill, my invaluable assistant, who has chased books and references and typed (late at night when there was no appealing movie on the television) two drafts of this book, I give the deepest and most heartfelt thanks.

DAVID M. WILSON
The British Museum
July 1983

1 Taste, personalities and survival

ENGLISH ART is and always has been eclectic, drawing for inspiration on its own traditions (often far back) and on such foreign influences as are immediate to English taste. Such was the case in the Christian Anglo-Saxon period when, through its eclecticism, English art laid strong foundations on which it was to build throughout its history. The influences taken into this art through the four centuries from 650 to 1050 (the period covered by this book) include such diverse tastes and motifs as those of the Romans, Italians, Gauls, Germans from beyond the Roman frontier, Byzantine churchmen, people loosely termed 'Celts' from Scotland and Ireland, Scandinavians of the Viking Age and even elements from the Arab world.

The period covered is long; it is as though we were to encompass in a similar volume the total history of English art from the middle years of the reign of Elizabeth I to the present day. The volume of available material is, however, of a very different character – meagre and often tenuously connected. Professor Dodwell, in an important and deeply considered book, has recently used this fact to express an opinion which contains much truth. 'The Anglo-Saxon arts which attract most attention today would have had little interest for the Anglo-Saxon writers. This is partly due to changes of taste but chiefly to accidents of survival.' He emphasizes that there have been enormous losses, particularly of gold and silver objects, which have distorted our whole impression of the art. The ravages of pirates, the rapaciousness of kings, the destructive zeal of architects, fire, the piety of clerics, ransom payments and many other causes have reduced the enormous wealth of English art in this period to a very low level. I can think of less than half-a-dozen metal objects of Anglo-Saxon manufacture that have remained above ground since the Anglo-Saxon period, and only one of those is of a secular nature – the Fuller Brooch, which has almost certainly never been buried.

At the same time much that is rich survives. Here the surviving material is represented in a manner somewhat different from that outlined by Dodwell, who has looked at the art of the period chiefly through the documents rather than through the objects. He has analysed the mentions of ornamented objects as they appear in the contemporary literature and revealed the massive – but now largely lost – wealth of Anglo-Saxon art; but this is the art as seen 'by the writers'. Much (sculpture, for example) does not appear in these literary descriptions: such omissions he explains partly because their materials were lacking in costliness or because writers 'did not often think in three-dimensional terms'. Although the great gold-adorned and jewelled images, the church plate and royal regalia and trappings are missing, much remains to tease the mind and even give a hint of the wealth that is lost. A true sequence of Anglo-Saxon art can, despite all the losses, be built up on the evidence of what survives.

2 *Opposite*: helmet from the Sutton Hoo ship-burial, Suffolk. Impressed copper plates are fixed to an iron cap. It is much restored. Height 31.8 cm. (London, British Museum)

1

3 Silver chalice from Trewhiddle, St Austell, Cornwall. The rim originally had an applied mount and this and the interior of the cup were gilt. Height 12.2 cm. (London, British Museum)

What the literature does show is the Anglo-Saxon love of colour – a factor clearly revealed in the art as it survives. It also reveals that *horror vacui* which is so obvious an element of the whole of Germanic art of the post-Roman period. No space could be left unornamented and when restraint leaves a surface only partially decorated the viewer can be surprised and even worried. Only on large objects like metal vessels do plain surfaces seem to be happily unadorned (the Trewhiddle Chalice, for example). Surfaces were often described in Old English poetry in terms which imply that an object glowed or shone or, more commonly, was bright. Dodwell has stressed how simple words like 'red', 'green' and 'yellow' are adorned by the poets with metaphor to emphasize life, colour and even movement. Precious stones were seen not merely as reflectors or transmitters, but rather as sources of light. The play of light on surfaces is often teased out into poetry. Pattern-welded swords, for example (that is weapons with blades of variegated colouring caused by hammering flat twisted case-hardened rods), are described as 'gleaming', 'serpent-like'. Sometimes colour can be imbued with deep meaning: Bede, for example, writes of colour thus:

> Just as in the pages of books we can represent both good and bad by any colour we like, without being censured, so in the matter of meanings, both good and bad can very properly be expressed by means of any human actions.

All the features admired and described by poets and writers are encountered in the material which survives. Sometimes triumphantly, as with the great Gospel Books; sometimes subtly, as in the use of gold inlaid in silver. Much, it is true, is now lost. Painting, for example. Fragments of painted wood are known and colour (mostly black and red) appears on stone sculpture – usually surviving only as a trace element, but occasionally still palely decorating the whole surface. A few pieces of wall plaster, a handful of embroidery, decorated leather-work, inlaid jewellery, wood inlaid with metal, metal laid on or in metal, gilding, tinning and enamelling survive to show the glitter, the surface movement, the busy-ness of the imagination of artist and craftsman. The Anglo-Saxons clearly craved glitter, colour and light. Glass for both window and table clearly demonstrates this deep-felt need; but for those who could not afford such luxuries, glass beads, polished wood, carved bone and gimcrack brooches were equally acceptable in creating an eye-teasing effect.

Much is missing from the surviving corpus of Anglo-Saxon art: decorated cushions, wall coverings, tapestries, bed hangings, panel paintings and painted furniture, for example. There is little in the way of decorated secular objects, other than jewellery; in particular we lack the dress of the richer secular classes, riches hinted at in finds of head bands and tunic borders in pagan Anglo-Saxon graves of an earlier period or in the few surviving pieces of ecclesiastical embroidery. A survey of Anglo-Saxon art has then to consider many imponderables, but with these lacunae as a background it is possible to build a structured survey of the historical sequence of the ornament and art of the period. What is more, the material considered here adds to our general knowledge of a shadowy period of English history and, through the manifestations of the creative spirit portrayed, we are able to appreciate the visual approach of the Anglo-Saxon to his man-made environment. We can appreciate also the craftsmanship and wealth available in the Anglo-Saxon world, gain a view of ideas of abstraction and humour, of tradition and curiosity, and of the influences which affected their culture and their eclectic creativity.

The coming of Christianity

This book deals with the art of the Christian Anglo-Saxons and much of the material discussed here has a religious character. A certain amount of secular art has been found, mostly by excavation; the Christian material has survived in churches and churchyards in much greater quantities. The story of the conversion of England has often been told, not least by Bede himself who had access to memory – however inaccurate – of at least some of the events. The story is not simple, and, although it need not concern us in detail, must be quickly summarized.

Augustine landed at Thanet in Kent in 597 with a band of missionaries, said by Bede to have numbered about forty. They came with the backing of Pope Gregory and seem to have been remarkably lucky and – initially at least – successful. Lucky in that Æthelbert, the king of Kent, was married to a Christian Frankish princess, which at least gave the mission an *entrée* into the royal household, and successful in that a letter to the patriarch of Alexandria from Gregory reports that 'At the feast of Christmas last year [597] more than ten thousand English are reported to have been baptized.' The Italian mission achieved further success; the king of Essex was converted, a see was erected in his capital, London, and a firm foothold for Christianity was for the time being established in south-east England. Æthelbert's death in 616 nearly smothered English Christianity, for his son was (at first) a pagan; Essex lapsed into apostasy and the bishop of London fled to Gaul. But the Christian missionaries persevered. Northumbria converted (for a time) and then East Anglia. Gradually Christianity was established despite the backsliding of many of the converted regions. After the death in battle of the great pagan king Penda in

4 Stirrup found in the River Thames at Battersea, London.
The pattern is effected by hammering copper wire into heavily scored iron, producing a glittering multicoloured surface. Height 23.9 cm. (London, British Museum)

11

655, the majority of the kingdoms of England became Christian; gradually other areas were mopped up, a process which culminated in the conquest and conversion of the pagan Isle of Wight, c.686.

By the 660s, when England was to all intents Christian, time was found to consolidate the diverse elements from which the English Church had been constructed. These comprised: the Italian tradition of Augustine; the Celtic tradition of the mission led by Aidan, which came to north-east England from the Scottish monastery of Iona after the accession of the Northumbrian king Oswy in 634; a Frankish tradition which had crept in as the old Italian missionaries had died off; an English tradition of the newly converted influenced from the Continent which produced some remarkable men (like Wilfrid, who was made bishop of the Northumbrians in 664); a native British tradition in the south-west which may well have been Christian before Augustine's mission and, lastly, the inspiration and genius of a prelate from Asia Minor, Theodore of Tarsus, appointed archbishop of Canterbury in 669.

Theodore was already old when he arrived in England, but he was to hold his see for twenty-one years and create authority within the Church across the political boundaries of the English kingdoms, from Northumbria to Wessex and from Kent to Mercia. Initially, the Church brought at least some temporary measure of ecclesiastical unity to England and with it a need for the trappings of the Church, the ornaments, plate, books, bells and hangings which were needed to enrich God's houses. This ecclesiastical unity is important in the study of the art since the contacts created throughout the various English kingdoms in artistic, scholarly and spiritual terms transcended political barriers. Although regionalism in art styles can often be recognized, such regionalism is not necessarily at all times politically significant. At the same time the art of the Church was eclectic, taking into itself influences from all the nationalities represented by the original missionaries and by the art of the people they had converted.

The old pagan religion gradually died away, its collapse reflected in the gradual disappearance of grave goods from the frequently encountered pagan cemeteries. Some cemeteries, like those excavated at Raunds, Northampton-shire, and Elstow, Bedfordshire, with numerous west–east oriented burials empty of accompanying grave goods, show the new Christian beliefs. But for a time there was a period of overlap. Some graves contained Christian objects: crosses, for example, and other symbolic signs of Christianity, like the fish on the belt buckle found at Crundale, Kent. Pagan Anglo-Saxon ornament is largely chronicled through the decoration on such objects and one of the more curious effects of Christianity on our knowledge of Anglo-Saxon England is the disappearance of one particular type of material – grave goods – characteristic of the fifth, sixth and seventh centuries.

Christianity and art

The Church introduced new media for the Anglo-Saxon artist, particularly stone sculpture and manuscript illumination. It is also possible that wall-painting was introduced by the Church; it was certainly much used in the decoration of their buildings, but it might have had a secular origin. Painting on wood had been known in the pagan period and there seems no reason to suppose that scenes as well as ornamental patterns were not produced by the pre-Christian artists of England; there is a tradition of painting – both narrative and ornamental – in the contemporary Germanic world. Wood-carving also survives from the Continent. Apart, however, from minor carving of small pieces of stone (the whetstone/sceptre from Sutton Hoo, for example) major sculpture was probably introduced into England as deliberate policy by the church builders of the middle years of the seventh century – perhaps from Gaul, whence for example Benedict Biscop had drawn the masons who built his new double monastery often referred to as Monkwearmouth/Jarrow, but perhaps depending in part on Italian or Byzantine traditions of small ivory or bone carving. Books were apparently unknown in England before the Conversion, although limited communication by runic writing was probably used before the Church landed pen in hand. The first books to reach England were Bibles and service books, presumably mainly from Italy whence came the first missionaries, but also probably from the major Gaulish religious houses, which provided hospitality for the travelling or fleeing missionary and for the newly converted pilgrims on their way to Rome or other sacred centres. A few books came from Ireland with the Celtic mission to the North.

But did the nature of the artist change with the coming of Christianity? In some ways the answer is Yes. The image and spirit of Christianity affected the artist's attitudes, while the patron of his work – secular or lay – may have dictated the subject of his produce. Some artists were certainly based in monasteries: Lindisfarne had a major *scriptorium* and metalworkers have been recognized through archaeology at Whitby, Monkwearmouth and Jarrow. Their presence in a Christian milieu must have influenced their art, but in general terms the deep-seated background of ancient Germanic taste continued to influence the artist's mind and consequently his product. This is particularly seen in the animal ornament which was to preoccupy part of the Anglo-Saxon artist's mind until the ninth century and even later. It is also to be seen in the *horror vacui* mentioned above, the urge to fill every space with ornament or colour in the manner so clearly encountered in pagan Anglo-Saxon metalwork.

Who were the artists?

The identity of the artist remains something of a mystery. Objects are occasionally signed. The Pershore censer, for example, bears an inscription, *Godric me wvorht[e]* (Godric made me), and simple statements of this nature are occasionally found elsewhere. The Lindisfarne Gospels has a long explanation of how it was produced:

> Eadfrith, bishop of the church at Lindisfarne originally wrote this book for God and St Cuthbert – jointly – for all the saints whose relics are in the island. And Ethilwald, bishop of the Lindisfarne islanders impressed it on the outside and covered it – as he well knew how to do. And Billfrith, the anchorite, forged the ornaments which are on it on the outside and adorned it with gold and with gems and also with gilded-over silver – pure metal. And Aldred, unworthy and most miserable priest, glossed it in English between the lines . . . Eadfrith, Ethilwald, Aldred made or, as the case may be, embellished this Gospel Book for God and Cuthbert.

This is a late addition to the manuscript, added in the tenth century, but it does suggest that the tradition of the original artists had lived on, and other manuscripts have similar statements; the Stockholm *Codex Aureus*, for example, mentions (with other monks) the goldsmith Wulfhelm. In

5 Terminal of the so-called sceptre or whetstone from Sutton Hoo. (London, British Museum)

101, 102

13

Æthelwulf's verse account of a cell of Lindisfarne he mentions an early eighth-century monk, Cwicwine, skilled in making iron vessels. But such references are rare and it is impossible to stretch the evidence for the monk-craftsman much further than their names.

By the very fact that most written records have an ecclesiastical origin it is clear that secular craftsmen are even more rarely mentioned; the names of clerics like Spearhafoc, abbot of Abingdon, and Mannig of Evesham, who appear in post-Conquest sources, are more elaborately (not to say fulsomely) described. Dodwell has produced evidence for teamwork under the leadership of such men in the making of shrines, like the great reliquary made for Winchester under the patronage of King Edgar, and has further shown that some at least of the assistants were laymen and not clerics. Secular goldsmiths have been traced working at Winchester, Barking and elsewhere and another, Leofwine, held land from the abbey of Abingdon; Æthelgifu, in the late tenth century, through her will releases her goldsmith, Mann, from bondage together with his wife and two sons. Some sources indicate skill in more than one craft – a goldsmith who also made swords is recorded in the will of the Atheling Athelstan (1015) where 'the sword with the silver hilt which Wulfric made, and the gold belt and the armlet which Wulfric made' are left to the church in which Athelstan is to be buried. (Archaeological evidence quite clearly shows that sword blades were often made by one smith and given their hilt by another.) The free status of some artists is demonstrated by a painter, Wulfroth, who held land in the second half of the tenth century in Northamptonshire and by a lay scribe who held land at Worcester in return for copying books for the monastery. It is clear then that there were both lay and clerical craftsmen and that the simplistic view that all scribes were monks is not true, nor indeed were all goldsmiths and jewellers members of the laity.

The scribe and the jeweller are the craftsmen most frequently encountered in the written sources; the sculptor in stone and the wood-carver are not mentioned, so we have no idea of the status of artists in these media, although we may assume that their rank was lower than that of goldsmiths. (Some sculptures, e.g. the tenth-century Alnmouth cross-shaft, do record a maker's name, but they are seldom informative.) While it is possible that noble ladies (both clerical and lay) may have indulged in fine embroidery there can be little doubt that people in humbler circumstances may have assisted them or even done the whole job (the semantics of the Latin word *fecit* (he made) would allow of both possibilities). Whether men were ever embroiderers is not clear.

We have seen that artists were both free and bonded, as well as members of religious orders. Some were attached, like Mann, to rich patrons; others were kept by kings and clerics (King Alfred had a number of craftsmen and Ælfwold, bishop of Crediton, had a scribe; other bishops were patrons of, or had in their households, many other craftsmen). But the craftsman/artist was not without honour or distinction; the sword-smith (because he held a man's life in his hands) and the goldsmith (because he dealt with precious metal) were the most prestigious craftsmen. One goldsmith is recorded in the Domesday Book as having even achieved the aristocratic status of thegn. It is not without interest that on the Sittingbourne dagger the maker's name is more prominent than that of the owner.

There is some evidence of incipient craft guilds by the end of the Anglo-Saxon period. Archaeological finds of metalworkers' waste, workshops and tools in such towns as Lincoln and York, together with street names in some cities implying crafts, demonstrate the banding together of craftsmen for trade, protection and convenience. English craftsmen-artists travelled abroad. Ninth- and eleventh-century records tell of English metalworkers and other craftsmen in foreign parts, just as there are mentions of continental artists in England from the period of Benedict Biscop in the seventh century onwards. The influence of English art on the Continent in the eighth and ninth centuries is clearly seen in the surviving material (see pp. 130ff.), just as the stone churches and sculpture of an earlier age reflect Gaulish influence in this country.

One well-documented class of craftsman is not discussed in this book, namely moneyers. Coins provide a fruitful area of stylistic analysis, but, with rare exceptions, show few distinctive or important ornamental traits. Recent finds in York have included moneyers' dies and trial pieces of the tenth century in an artisans' quarter in Coppergate, where there are traces of metalworking and other crafts. It should, however, be remembered that moneyers presumably had a great deal to do with silversmiths – both as clients and customers – from the late eighth century onwards, the period when the English silver coinage came of age.

Dating

The dating of the art of the Christian Anglo-Saxon period is not easy. There are few absolute dates. To a large extent the historian of the subject depends on the study of the development and degeneration of style: a method which can hardly be deemed accurate. No object signed by an artist of known date survives. Some objects however are associated with artists by later inscription (as the Lindisfarne Gospels), others are associated with known historical personages, either by inscription (e.g. the rings of Æthelswith and Æthelwulf) 117, 118 or by their presence in the tomb of a known person (e.g. St Cuthbert's cross). Objects found in coin hoards can be dated before the latest coin in the find (e.g the Trewhiddle silver); other objects have an earliest possible date for their 119 production (e.g. the New Minster Charter, which must have been written after the foundation of the New Minster at Winchester). Palaeography is often a help in dating a manuscript, particularly where groups of scribes are well defined (consider the Lindisfarne group, pp. 36–49, for example), but epigraphy rarely helps and orthography seldom. Modern methods of dating by the radio-carbon method and by the analysis of tree-rings have made hardly any inroads into the dating of the art of this period. Such methods are potentially of use, however, particularly in placing material found during excavations in a definite chronological context. The radio-carbon method is (particularly for this period, in which there are large margins of error) a very crude means of dating an object, while the full tree-ring series for dating hard woods in this country is not yet complete back to the Roman period and, even when it is complete, it will take many years to apply the accurate dates obtained through this method to archaeological deposits containing decorated objects – in most foreseeable cases it is not the objects themselves, but the contexts in which they are found, which will be datable by tree-ring analysis.

Despite all these reservations it is fair to say that there is a considerable body of accepted common ground among specialists which allows the erection of a reasonable chronology for Anglo-Saxon art. Only in the vast field of Anglo-Saxon sculpture is stylistic judgement almost the sole means of building up a chronology, although even here there are some fixed points (the settlement of the Vikings, for example, or the incorporation of a stone in a building of known date) which enable us to erect a very coarse chronological scale.

6 Gold buckle with niello inlay from Sutton Hoo.
Length 13 cm. (London, British Museum)

Sutton Hoo

The origins of much Anglo-Saxon art of the Christian period are clearly seen in pagan Anglo-Saxon grave-goods. It is not my intention to delve too deeply into these origins, but the greatest of all Anglo-Saxon graves, Sutton Hoo No. 1, forms not only a convenient corpus of material for investigation of the origins of Christian art, but also shows many of the influences which went into its construction. It is so closely related to some of the earliest Christian material that a summary of the artistic context of the grave is essential to an understanding of the art of the later seventh and eighth centuries.

The Sutton Hoo ship-burial was excavated in 1939 and produced one of the richest treasures ever found in England. It seems likely that a body was buried in the grave (although no trace of it survived, due to the acid nature of the soil). The accompanying grave-goods are of a remarkable and special – presumably royal – quality. Some are imports (in themselves demonstrating the foreign connections of the Anglo-Saxon peoples): silver and bronze vessels from the eastern Mediterranean; a shield from Sweden; a sword-pommel which almost certainly comes from the Rhineland; coins from Merovingian Gaul; two silver spoons of Byzantine type and a dish stamped with control marks of the Byzantine emperor Anastasius. Also included in the grave were three bronze hanging-bowls, the enamelled mounts of which are decorated with spiral ornament and embellished with *millefiori* mosaic. The bowls may (or may not) be Anglo-Saxon, but the ornament of the mounts is of importance in the development of later Anglo-Saxon art. Other ornamented objects are all of English origin – even the helmet is now seen to have Anglo-Saxon parallels. Ornament is found in many contexts; on drinking horns, cups, weapons, on

8, 9

2

16

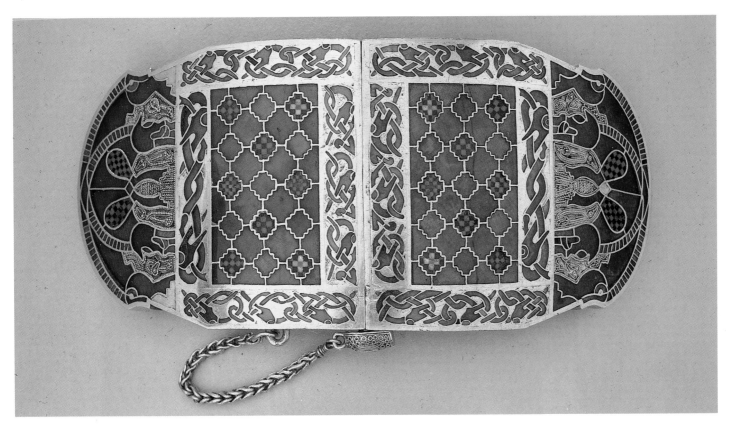

7 Shoulder clasp from Sutton Hoo.
Length 11.8 cm (London, British Museum).
See pp. 16, 25

8, 9 Mount (diameter 5.5 cm) from the base of a
hanging bowl and (*right*) plaque (width 5.5 cm) from its
side. From Sutton Hoo.
Both mounts are inlaid with enamel, which in turn is
inlaid with *millefiori*, offcuts from a multicoloured rod
of glass set end on (London, British Museum). See pp.
16, 25

10, 11 Two pages from a Gospel Book. (Durham, Cathedral Library, A.II.10, ff. 2ʳ and 3ᵛ). *Left*, the colophon at the end of St Matthew's Gospel; *right*, the beginning of St Mark. Height 38.5 cm. See pp. 32, 33

Marci

INCIPIT

a euuang
eli ihu xpi fili
di sicut scriba
est inaesaia
propheta ec
ce mitto ang
elum meum ante faciem
tuam qui praeparabit
uiatuam ·:· Uox claman
tis indeserto parate uiā
dni rectas facite semitas
eius ·:· fuit iohannis in
deserto baptizans et
praedicans baptismum
paenitentiae etremission
empeccatorum etegredie
batur adillum omnis iudeae
regio ethienusolimite uniuersi et
baptizabantur abillo inionda
ne etconfitentes peccata sua
et erat iohannis uestitus py
lis cameli etzona pellicia emea
lumbos eius etlocusta etmellsil ue
uescae aedebat etpraedicabat
dicens uenit fortior post me cu
ius honsum dignus procumbens
soluere conrigiam calciamento
rum eius ego baptizaui uos inaq
ua ille baptizabit uos inspiritu
sco ·:· et factum est indieb.
illis uenit iohannis anazareth
galileae etbaptizatus est
iniondane abiohanne etstatim
ascendens deaqua uidit ape
rtos et caelos etspm tanquam
columbam discendentem etma
nentem inipso etuox facta est
adeum decaelis tu es filius meus
dilectus inte conplacui ·:· et
statimsps expulit eum indeser
to eratibi xl. diebus etxl noct
bus ettemptabatur asatan et
erat cumbestis etangeli mi
nistrabant ei ·:· Post autem

traditus est iohannis uenit ihs in
galeam praedicans euangelium regni
di adicens quoniam impletum est tempus
etadpropinquauit regnum di peni
temini etcredite euangelio etpraetere
uens secus mare galileae uidit sizo
nem etandream fratrem eius mitten
tes retia inmare erant enim pis
catores ·:· et dixit eis ihs
uenite post me etfaciam
uos fieri piscatores ho
minum et continuo ne
lictis retib. secutisunt eum
etprogresus inde pussillumul
dit iacobum ze bedei etiohannen
fratrem eius ·:· et ipsos innaui
conponentes retia etstatim uocauit
illos etrelicto patre suo zebedeo in
naui cum mercinaris secuti sunt eum
et ingrediuntur capharnaum et
statim sabbatis ingresus sinagoga
docebat eos ·:· et stupebant sup
doctrinam eius erat enim docens
quasi potestatem habens ethonsicut
scribae ·:· et erat insinagoga eorum
homo inspu inmundo etexclamauit
dicens haec quid nobis ettibi ihu na
zarene uenisti perdere nos scio qu
esses dei etcomminatusest ei ihdicens
etobmutasce etexi dehomine spsim
mundus et cum sps immundus dis
perseum etexclamauit uoce magna
exiuit abeo etmirati sunt omnes
ita ut conquirerent interse dicentes
quidnam est hoc quae doctrina
noua quia inpotestate etspiriti
bus inmundis imperat etoboediu
ei etprocessit rumor eius statim in
omnem regionem galileae ·:· et pr
imus egrediens desinagoga uenerunt
indomum simonis et andreae cum
iacobo et iohanne ·:· socrus autem si
monis febricitans et statim dicunt
de illa etaccedens ele
uauit eam adpraehensa manu
eius etcontinuo dimisit eam febris
etministrabat eis ·;·

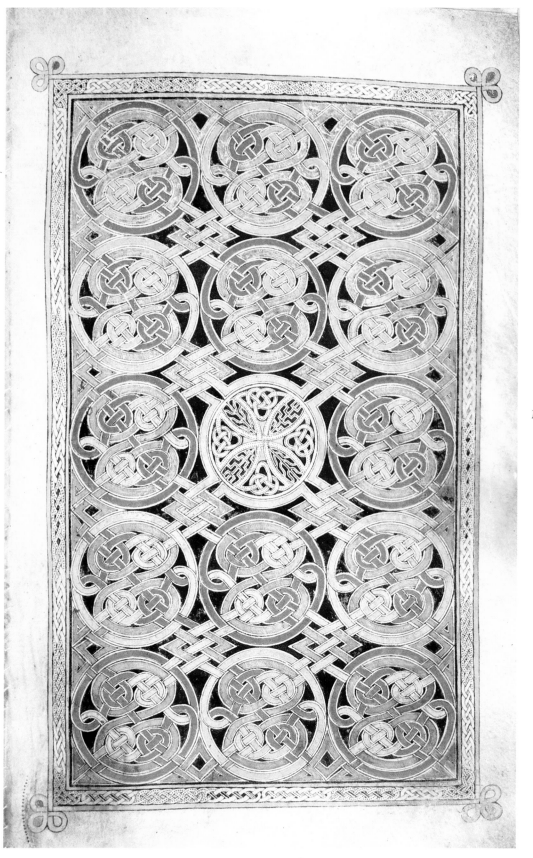

12, 13 Two facing pages from the Book of Durrow (Dublin, Trinity College Library, A.4.5.(57), ff. 85v and 86r). *Left*, an ornamental carpet page; *right*, the beginning of St Mark. 24.5 × 14.5 cm. See pp. 33–5

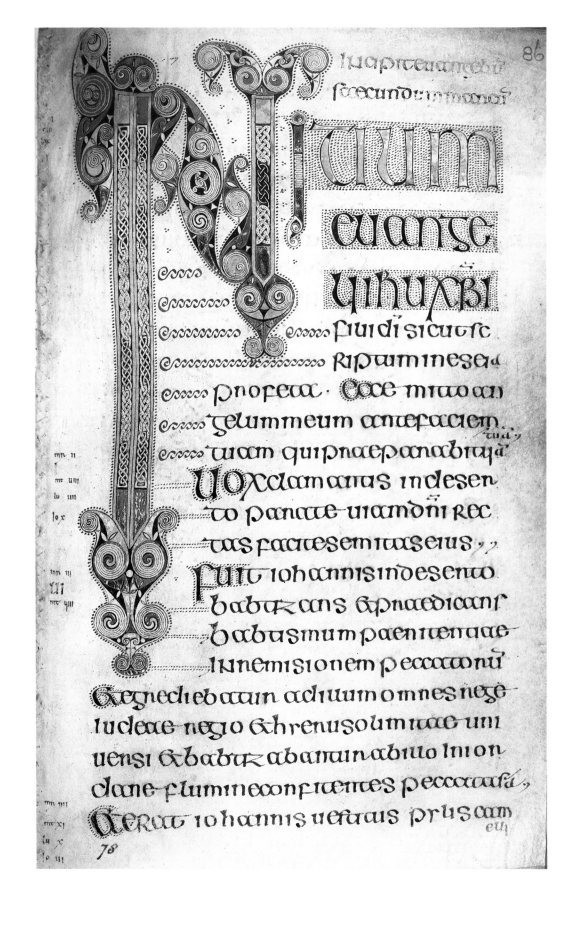

Incipit euangelii
secundum marcum

Tium
euange
lii ihuxbi

fiui di sicut sc
riptum in esa
propheta · ecce mitto an
gelum meum ante faciem
uiam qui praeparabit uia
uox clamantis in desen
to parate uiam dni rec
tas facite semitas eius
fuit iohannis in deserto
babtizans et praedicans
babtismum paenitentiae
in remisionem peccatorum
et egrediebatur ad illum omnes rege
iudeae regio et hrenusolimitae uni
uensi et babtizabantur ab illo in ion
dane flumine confitentes peccata sua
erat iohannis uestitus pilis cam

14 The symbol of St Mark, from the Echternach Gospels (Paris, Bibliothèque Nationale, lat.9389, fol. 75v). 33.5 × 25.5 cm. See pp. 36, 38

15 Portrait and symbol of St Luke, with scenes from his Gospel, from the so-called St Augustine Gospels (Cambridge, Corpus Christi College, 286, fol. 129v). 24.5 × 18 cm. See p. 29

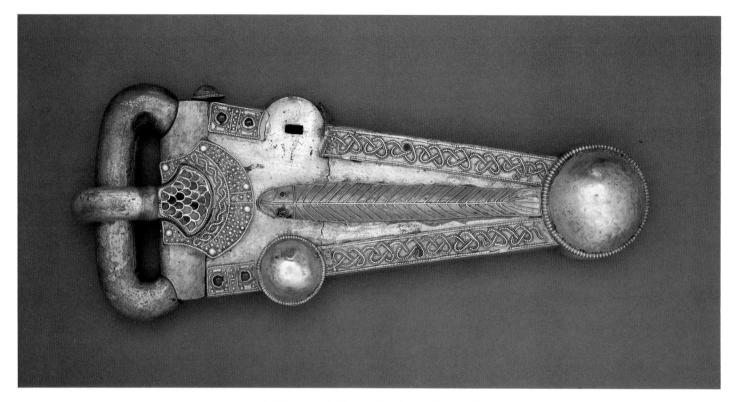

16 Silver parcel-gilt belt buckle, possibly a reliquary
buckle, from Crundale, Kent.
It bears the Christian symbol of the fish. Length 15.2 cm
(London, British Museum). See p. 12

17 Cross from the tomb of St
Cuthbert, Durham Cathedral.
Width 6 cm (Durham, Cathedral
Treasury). See p. 29

18 Cross, said to be from Wilton,
Norfolk.
Width 4.8 cm (London, British
Museum). See p. 29

the 'sceptre' and (of most relevance in this context) on a great deal of personal jewellery. The coins in the burial were assembled at some time after 622 and it is usually assumed that it was a king who was buried here and that he was Rædwald, king of East Anglia, who died in 625. In my opinion Sigeberht (died 635) or possibly Eorpwald (died either c.627 or 632) were more probably buried in the Sutton Hoo grave, but the matter is, from the art-historical point of view, of minimal importance. What is clear is that we have a terminal date between say 625 and 635 for the deposit of the objects buried in the grave. Much of the material must, therefore, have been made within a generation before these dates. Further, the bulk of the personal jewellery seems to have been made in one workshop by a craftsman of exceptional brilliance. It is work of the highest quality, not only in English but in European terms.

Apart from the technical excellence of the craftsmanship, the use of colour is the most striking feature of the jewellery. It is all of gold and is inlaid with various materials. Only the great gold buckle is inlaid with niello, but most of the jewellery is inlaid with garnets (it is estimated that there are some 4,000 individually cut garnets in the find) and with subtly coloured pieces of *millefiori* glass each of which forms a chequer pattern of blue and white or red and white. The jewelled surfaces give an impression of a highly polished miniature mosaic, glittering with reds and gold, occasionally relieved by blue and white. The translucent materials are mostly backed with gold foil impressed with geometrical patterns which reflect light back through the garnets or glass to give a glittering and lively appearance to the surface, adding to the articulated impression implicit in the general division of the fields into multicoloured cells. Here we encounter the glistening colour-brightness which so fascinated the Anglo-Saxon writers of a later period, with their particular interest in reddish tones. This was the colour which added life to the drabness of natural colours and the dyes of cloth and wood.

The glittering mosaic quality is best exemplified on the pair of clasps, unique in form, which are the most perfectly composed objects in the find. Each clasp is joined by a central hinge, and the halves can be separated by the withdrawal of the hinge pin (itself embellished with an animal-headed terminal). On the backs of each clasp are a series of loops which allow them to be sewn on to a garment, presumably at the shoulders. At either end of each clasp is a pattern composed of a pair of interlocking boars. The spaces between the bodies of each animal are filled with filigree (itself of zoomorphic character) and, apart from the front hips, the bodies are completely filled with garnets, the outlines being formed of the edges of the cells which hold the garnets. The hips are worked in a pattern of blue, white and red *millefiori* glass. The tusks of the boars on one half of one pair of clasps are of blue glass. Behind the garnets patterned foils reflect and refract the light back through the stones at different angles. The patterns of the foil vary; that behind the garnets of the boars' backbones is different from that used in their bodies (it is interesting that the major grid lines of the foil behind the cells which form the bodies are set at different but complementary angles); further, there is an apparently deliberate attempt on one of the clasps to select the stones to give a different tone of red to the backbones of the animals. The gems are cut with great accuracy and, in the major fields of the body, are of considerably greater size than is normal in contemporary jewellery in England or on the Continent, where the technique had its origins.

6

7

19

25

7   The main field of each clasp is rectangular in form. Set in a plain gold border are panels of interlaced animals with ribbon-like bodies which vary in detail but are substantially the same in style and form. The bodies are inlaid with garnets, the eye being of pale blue. Although in technique these animals are unique they belong to a stylistic family common to Germanic Europe. They appear in a more elaborate and varied form on the massive gold buckle from Sutton Hoo, where they are produced in a cast technique which has its origins in woodworker's chip-carving, but here expressed with consummate artistry. Distinguished as 'Style II' by Bernhard Salin in 1904 in his classic study of the development of Germanic animal art, animals with ribbon-like bodies (usually with interlacing limbs and jaws) occur throughout Europe from Scandinavia to Italy in slightly varying forms from the end of the sixth century until well into the seventh century. In England, as will be shown, this style develops into a very different form as the century progresses and the new techniques of manuscript painting and sculpture appear. On the Continent it also takes different turnings, although in Scandinavia it appears to run in a continuous, but developing, sequence until well on into the eighth century. The animals form, however, a strong and developing element in the art which concerns us here. They have an ultimate origin in earlier Germanic styles which were developed on the northern edges of the Roman Empire c.A D 400 and, by the time we encounter them at Sutton Hoo, they may have lost their meaning or, if they did retain any meaning, we cannot understand it today, although attempts are made from time to time to endow them with attributes from heroic legend. They are an essential element of the Anglo-Saxon ornamental

19   tradition: the drawings here analyse their structure, bringing out the details of leg, head, and body.

The centre of each main field of the Sutton Hoo clasps forms a carpet-like pattern of interlocking, step-sided cells, filled with garnets and *millefiori* glass. This is the ultimate achievement of a technique of Germanic cloisonné work which is again common to Germanic Europe, appearing first in the fifth century in areas as widely dispersed as Romania and Scandinavia. The cloisonné technique has a unique interest in England in that jewellery of this type may well be the inspiration for some of the so-called 'carpet pages' of many great Gospel Books of the seventh and eighth centuries (see below, p. 38).

There are many pieces of cloisonné garnet jewellery from Sutton Hoo, but the clasps are perhaps the most important and certainly the most relevant to the theme of this book. The wealth of the grave is not, however, confined to the jewellery. Three bronze basins of a type known as 'hanging-bowls' were discovered in the grave deposit and it is convenient to use the largest of these to introduce an element of Christian Anglo-Saxon art which is at once important and controversial, namely the champlevé enamelling of spirals and other motifs. The bowl was suspended by three hooks at the rim; cast in one with the hooks are circular panels inlaid with cuprite glass (loosely termed enamel) of

8, 9   different colours. There are five other inlaid plaques on this, the largest of the Sutton Hoo hanging-bowls (it is 31 cm in diameter). The patterns on them are basically spiraliform, and the plain colours of the fused glass are enlivened by the introduction of multi-coloured *millefiori* into the pattern. The spirals take various forms, producing peltas and trumpet-like terminals which run into one another with great delicacy. Although the form of the spiral ornament appears

26

to be complicated, the basic structure of the conjoined spiral patterns (both here and in later and more elaborate manifestations) is subject to little variation. The pattern is only complicated by the method in which the individual elements are made to join with each other. In later examples the use of individual spirals linked to others drawn on a different scale adds to the apparent complexity of the pattern, but in reality spirals comprise one of the less complicated pattern structures of Anglo-Saxon art. The main colour used on the Sutton Hoo bowl is red; but blue and pale green are also used, as well as blue glass inlays.

The spiral style so competently utilized on the Sutton Hoo hanging-bowls is the product of a long history which reaches back to the pre-Roman Iron Age. Celtic artists developed it and somehow (perhaps in Ireland, perhaps in Scotland, perhaps in England or even in all three countries) spiral enamelling survived and began to flower again in the late sixth century. Few objects have been found in dated contexts but it is clear that the style was alive in Ireland and Scotland and great controversy has surrounded the origins of the more than one hundred and fifty known hanging-bowls. This is not the place to enter into a discussion of this complicated problem as it is of only marginal importance in the context of this book. Suffice it to say that the generally received opinion now seems to be that hanging-bowls with enamelled escutcheons like the large Sutton Hoo example were being produced in Northumbria, west Britain and Scotland by the seventh century in the areas which were to become influenced by the Celtic Church. It should also be said that enamelling is rarely found in England after the seventh century, but was much used in Ireland and to a lesser extent in Pictland (basically eastern and northern Scotland) where a particular feature at this point was the introduction of yellow enamel, possibly from England.

An element foreign to much Anglo-Saxon art of the pagan and Conversion period – the naturalistic portrayal of the human figure – is rare at Sutton Hoo. Semi-naturalistic scenes occur in small panels on the helmet and there are heads on the whetstone/sceptre which are merely formalized abstractions. This struggle to represent the human figure will be seen throughout our consideration of Anglo-Saxon Christian art. Occasionally, as in the later stone sculpture, the artist succeeds in portraying – or almost succeeds in portraying – the human figure, but it is not until the tenth century that consistently competent human representation is achieved. Have we here perhaps a trace of a pagan taboo against the naturalistic representation of the human form or a relic of a pagan iconoclasm? Unfortunately we cannot step into the mind of the patron or artist in the pagan period; we can only look at it with incomplete knowledge from outside. The idea of accurate or even ideal portrayal is still far from the mind (or the achievement?) of the Anglo-Saxon artist as Christianity begins to affect his thinking.

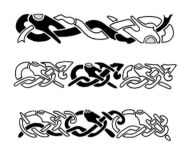

19 Analysis of the animal ornament on one of the Sutton Hoo shoulder clasps. See pl. 7

5

2 The seventh-century explosion

THAT THE CHURCH took over the art and the techniques of the pagan Anglo-Saxon craftsman should cause no surprise; this is nowhere more clearly demonstrated than by an object found in the reliquary coffin of St Cuthbert in Durham Cathedral. Among the undoubted personalia of St Cuthbert deposited in the original burial of this great churchman, who died on 20 March 687, was his pectoral cross, which was old (perhaps as much as thirty years old) and damaged when it was placed in the grave. This cross – symbol of the new religion – is in a direct line of descent from the pagan Anglo-Saxon jewellery of which Sutton Hoo provides the richest evidence. It is of gold and garnet, 6 cm across, with expanded arms, square cells and with a white shell base to the central circular element. Its workmanship is almost coarse compared with Sutton Hoo (it has simple rather heavy cells and no foil beneath the garnets) but it also is rich and glowing. Other crosses of an earlier period from Wilton, Norfolk (probably from the Sutton Hoo workshop), and from Ixworth, Suffolk, are also ornamented with garnets, and other finds in 'pagan'-type graves show that there was a fashion for wearing such objects in the seventh century. Jewellery of this period is rarely encountered (Christianity had eroded the pagan custom of burial with accompanying grave goods) but St Cuthbert's cross serves to remind us of the continuing tradition of the jeweller's art as we turn to consider the more heady manuscript remains.

The first books

The Church at the time of the Conversion needed books, particularly service books and Bibles. Initially at least, the missionaries' wants were supplied by gifts from neighbouring Christian countries, but soon books were being copied for home consumption. Many books presumably did not survive medieval neglect, but many remained in the monasteries until the English Reformation. Fortunately there were some bibliophiles around at the time of the Dissolution of the Monasteries who, through agents, enriched themselves and posterity from the great monastic libraries. Such a person was Matthew Parker, Master of Corpus Christi College, Cambridge, from 1544 to 1553 and archbishop of Canterbury from 1559 to his death in 1575. In 1568 he was given authority by the Privy Council to collect manuscripts from the monasteries and most of them (the majority from Canterbury itself) went to the library of his old college, where they remain to this day. His collection contains a book which reputedly came to England with the Christian missionaries (Cambridge, Corpus Christi College, 286), the so-called St Augustine Gospels, still produced for the enthronement of successive archbishops of Canterbury, as well as a Gospel Book (MS.197 B) written either in Ireland or Northumbria within a century of the mission. Parker was interested in the history of the English Church and its relation to the original Church of the Anglo-Saxon

20 *Opposite*: front cover of the Stonyhurst Gospel. Red leather. The incised lines are inlaid with black and yellow pigment and the plant scroll is moulded over string or leather. 13.8 × 9.2 cm. (On loan to the British Library, London, from Stonyhurst College)

17

18

15

29

period; he thus collected books containing sermons, chronicles, theological works and biographies, as well as poetry, service books and Bibles. His was the most varied and greatest of the collections of Anglo-Saxon manuscripts formed at the Reformation; other collections were more crudely put together out of curiosity or for historical or theological purposes. As a result of the activities of Parker and his contemporaries a large number of books survive from the Anglo-Saxon period. Of the early Anglo-Saxon books generally only the great service books and Bibles are illuminated, though as early as the mid-eighth century there are, for example, illustrated versions of Cassiodorus's commentary on the psalms (Durham, Cathedral Library, B.II.30) and of Bede's *Ecclesiastical history of the English nation* (Leningrad, Public Library, Cod. Q.v.I.18). Later, particularly in the tenth and eleventh centuries, illustrated books of a secular or semi-secular nature become more common.

It is easy in a discussion of art to forget that some books were meant for study and meditation, and others for use publicly as service books. The important element was the text, the illumination was embellishment. Many manuscripts went unilluminated: charters, wills and other legal documents, for example. Some manuscripts are so beautifully written that illumination would seem only to spoil them (the Stonyhurst Gospel, for example – one of the few Anglo-Saxon books, incidentally, to preserve its original binding), but most of the grander books have at least slightly embellished initials, sometimes merely filled with a wash of colour. The script used in the first centuries of English book production was derived from Mediterranean prototypes. The main book-hand was uncial (a term of obscure origin) which has its roots in Roman cursive script and which was at its best in fifth-century Italy. Its elegance is comprised in its curved strokes, its roundness. There are two forms of script, majuscule and minuscule. To use Lowe's phrase, 'in general majuscule differs from minuscule in being rounder, more solid, more stately. . . A style for grand manuscripts.' It is not the purpose of this book to describe in detail the scripts of the Anglo-Saxons. Suffice it to say that the scripts are elegant and produced with skill, and that regional and chronological differences enable the palaeographer on general stylistic grounds to assign the manuscripts to a particular area or period.

The first books produced in England were written in the uncial script which had been used in books like the St Augustine Gospels (then probably in Canterbury) or the Burchard Gospels (Würzburg, Universitätsbibliothek, M.P.Th.F.68), which was then in Northumbria. But another (non-uncial) tradition is also perceived in these first manuscripts, namely that of Irish script. Four ornamented early seventh-century books produced in Irish or Irish-influenced continental *scriptoria* are known. Two of these, the Ussher Gospels (Dublin, Trinity College, A.4.15(55)) and the Cathach of St Columba (Dublin, Royal Irish Academy, S.n), are the most important. The Ussher Gospels, probably the earliest surviving book produced in the British Isles, has on one leaf a reddish-brown cross framed by three simple borders. This is perhaps a harbinger of the great carpet pages produced in England and Ireland at a later period. The Cathach must belong to the first half of the seventh century and is important in the history of insular art – the art of the British Isles – in that here can be perceived for the first time in the surviving material that elaboration of initial letters which was to become such an important element in Anglo-Saxon manuscript art, together with the trick of diminution, by which a large initial

31

54, 55

20

15

21

21 *Opposite*: page from an Irish psalter, the Cathach of St Columba (Dublin, Royal Irish Academy, S.n)

...gur e nomen eius...

DS IN adiutorium meum intende
dne : ad adiuuandum me festina
confundantur & reuereantur qui quaerunt
animam meam / uolunt mihi mala
auertantur retrorsum & erubescant qui
uolentantur statim erubescentes
qui dicunt mihi euge euge
exsultent & laetentur in te omnes qui quaerunt te
& dicant semper magnificetur ds
qui diligunt salutare tuum
ego uero egenus & pauper ds adiuua me
adiutor meus & liberator meus es tu dne ne moreris

IN te dne speraui non confundar in aeternum
in iustitia tua libera me et eripe me
inclina ad me aurem tuam et salua me
esto mihi in dm protector et in
locum munitum ut saluum me facias

letter is followed by letters of gradually reducing size at the start of an important passage (in this case the first line of each psalm). The ornament of the initials is an integral part of the design of the page; peltas, spirals and animal-heads are introduced as embellishment and the lines of text are planned in relation to them.

Irish and Anglo-Saxon centres developed methods of book production distinct from those of the Continent. The vellum used for the pages has a suede-like finish quite unlike the polished surface of continental vellum; the gathering of quires, often the ruling of the sheets and perhaps even the form of the binding also differentiate the insular books. For this reason it is clear that, as many of these traits and the ornamental ones mentioned above are first found in Ireland, English books were influenced by Ireland as well as by the Continent. This is hardly surprising. From the Scottish monastery of Iona (founded from Ireland *c.*563) St Aidan came in 635 under royal patronage to found the great Northumbrian monastery of Lindisfarne, which was soon to become a centre of learning and art with a continuing link with Columban Ireland. Two Christian traditions, Latin and Celtic, met here and, even after the Synod of Whitby in 664, which resulted in the partial withdrawal of the Celtic Church from England, there was sufficient contact with the west to keep the Irish influence in the north of England refreshed.

It is, then, something of a shock to encounter the earliest Anglo-Saxon illuminated manuscript, the fragment of a Gospel Book in Durham Cathedral
10, 11   Library (A.II.10). Instead of the rather insignificant and almost casual decoration of the surviving Irish manuscripts we are presented with elaborate, finely finished, large-scale ornament in positive colours. The decoration of the colophon (the tailpiece) of St Matthew's Gospel shows a competence of composition and an assurance of touch that foreshadows the great ornamented manuscripts which follow it. Ranged down the right-hand side of the page are three D-shaped fields joined by a frame. The spaces between the frame and the hoops of the Ds are filled with ribbon interlace in yellow, blue and red and the angles of the field towards the corners of the page are finished with an elaboration of a spiralled pelta. The hoops of the Ds are filled with varying forms of interlace in yellow. Each ribbon carries a double line of dots (as indeed does all the ribbon interlace on this page). The colophon which filled the three main fields is now faded. The opening page of St Mark's Gospel has the same colour range. In the left column the monogram INI stretches down two-thirds of the left-hand margin: the oblique element of the letter N is made up of ribbon interlace terminating in simple animal heads: spirals and peltas complete the ornament. The rest of the first line follows the diminution of the letters encountered in the Cathach, but the letters themselves are decorated only with minor flourishes or emphasized wedges.

What is surprising about Durham A.II.10 is that it is so advanced, so well-formed. It is both disciplined and asymmetric. The beginnings of the Anglo-Saxon artist's subtlety are to be seen in the different designs of the interlace in the frames of each of the D-shaped fields. Each pattern is different, but superficially they look similar. This is a feature encountered with great sophistication at a later period in the Book of Durrow and the Lindisfarne Gospels. The origins of the ornamental motifs used here have been much discussed. The pelta motif, although clearly of Celtic origin (as is the trumpet development of the initials in one diminishing line), could have been taken directly from Northumbrian-made hanging-bowls. The interlace is akin to that which appears on the Sutton Hoo buckle-loop and it is not without interest that, like other parts of the Sutton Hoo buckle, the ribbons are dotted. In fact the ornament of the three D-shaped loops might well be based on the designs of seventh-century nielloed gold. It is sometimes said that the other colours used in the manuscript reflect enamelling techniques. This is open to question (blue and red are two of the simplest colours available to the scribe) but we shall meet similar parallels below.

There is, then, in Durham A.II.10 a synthesis of Celtic and Anglo-Saxon ornament. Palaeographers agree that it was made in Northumbria, under Irish influence, about the middle of the seventh century, although a few art-historians hanker after an Irish origin. If it was produced in Northumbria – as seems almost certain – we cannot say where it was made. Its presence at Durham in the fourteenth century might suggest that it was written at Lindisfarne (Durham was the ultimate successor of Lindisfarne as owner of the patrimony of St Cuthbert) or was at some time in Lindisfarne.

The Book of Durrow

The problem of the Irish or English origins of objects and of style in seventh-century England is nowhere more problematic than in the discussion of the Book of Durrow (Dublin, Trinity College, A.4.5.(57)), the earliest surviving fully illuminated insular manuscript. The manuscript takes its name from an Irish monastery in Co. Offaly founded by St Columba, who died c.597; the manuscript was almost certainly there in the late 11th or early 12th century when a document concerning the monastery was written on its last leaf. But its history before then is unknown. There is no doubt that Durrow was an important monastery in the period in which the Book of Durrow was produced, but whether the book was produced there is a matter of much controversy: palaeographers in general assigning it to Northumbria and one or two art-historians saying it is Irish. A few scholars hedge their bets and consign it to Iona. Everybody now agrees that it was written in the second half of the seventh century in the period between Durham A.II.10 and the Lindisfarne Gospels. Most scholars assign it to a Northumbrian *scriptorium*.

First, the manuscript itself. It measures 24.5 × 14.5 cm, has 248 folios and is decorated throughout. It has six pages of overall ornament – carpet pages – a page bearing the symbols or personifications of the four Evangelists, a page with a single such symbol before each Gospel and six grand initials. There are also five pages of canon tables (tables of concordance between the different Gospels). The text is carefully written and most pages have one or two lines with embellished letters followed by the familiar diminution of the following characters to mark an important part of the text. Some initials are embellished with spiraliform terminals, some merely with dots, and there are seven major decorated initials in the preliminary matter. The ornament is made up of three main elements – interlace, spirals and animals – as well as representations of the Evangelist symbols. The main colours are yellow, orangey-red, black, white and green.

The carpet pages are the most startling innovations in the manuscript. Their origins have been much discussed. Two of the pages include a cross in the design, a feature found in Gospel Books in the Mediterranean world. Specific examples have been suggested as prototypes, particularly by Nordenfalk and

12, 13
22–25

22 Symbol of St Matthew, from the Book of Durrow (Dublin, Trinity College, A.4.5.(57), fol. 21v)

Schapiro; while these suggestions cannot be ignored, it is not impossible to see the origin of the carpet pages nearer to home: we have already noticed that the Ussher Gospels has a cross set in a frame and it may be that the Durrow carpet pages were a casual development of the insular area. Nor should it be forgotten that the rectangular panels of the Sutton Hoo clasps have an effect – in miniature – very similar to the carpet pages of the great Gospel Books. It seems entirely acceptable to propose an insular origin for these pages based on metalwork and jewellery prototypes, and to ignore the far-flung – and rather slim – parallels in the Mediterranean region offered as a solution. We shall see that elsewhere in the Book of Durrow there are noteworthy analogies to the Sutton Hoo material, while much of the other detail of the manuscript, as will be shown, is based on metalworkers' or jewellers' models.

The artist makes skilful use of his patterns and his colours. First he constructs a pattern and then he breaks it up into fields by changing the colour register, so that there are two ways of looking at the result. At the same time he gives an impression of false symmetry by following certain lines of construction, but misleads the eye by the use of different colour on the same ribbon. The same trick is used on the one carpet page, which is filled with spirals, and in the initials, which are mostly embellished with spiraliform designs. The asymmetry seen in these patterns is well exemplified earlier in the asymmetry of the ornament in the centre of the Sutton Hoo buckle, which at first glance looks well balanced beccuse of the framing animals. The Sutton Hoo buckle provides animals which are clearly of the same family as those which occur on the one carpet page with zoomorphic ornament. It has frequently been pointed out that the animals in the side panels of the page are almost exactly the same as that at the butt-end of the Sutton Hoo buckle. The design is so close that one wonders how as much as fifty years may separate them (perhaps it does not!). Here, however, can be seen the continuity of the Anglo-Saxon zoomorphic tradition into the Christian period.

The remaining elements of the ornament of the Book of Durrow are the representations of the Evangelists which here make their first appearance in insular art. Their origins have been much discussed with little result. The symbols appear without haloes and wings, unlike the symbols in the Lindisfarne Gospels and their many successors in insular art. The St Matthew symbol demonstrates the artist's complete unfamiliarity with human representation in art and has been aptly described as 'a walking buckle'. Indeed the whole cloak appears to be made up of garnets and *millefiori* glass within a metal frame. Is it possible that the artist, who I believe to have been partly schooled in a metalworking centre, had no model for the evangelist symbols, knew of a formula and did his best? The animal symbols are much more competently, if not naturalistically, constructed but then the Anglo-Saxon artist knew about animal ornament. Isabel Henderson has suggested, and recently confirmed her belief, that the lion symbol is derived from Pictish art. I cannot accept this thesis and agree with Robert Stevenson that the derivation is the other way round. The metalworking quality of the ornament in the Book of Durrow shows the roots of these motifs and the chronological position of the manuscript and its ornamental prototypes in metalwork seem to support Stevenson's arguments. Indeed it is possible to see in Isabel Henderson's most recent work a tendency to be a little more elastic towards Stevenson's suggestion. Whatever the case, there is undoubtedly a connection

34

23 Comparison of animal motifs from the Sutton Hoo buckle (*left*; see pl. 6) and the Book of Durrow (*right*)

24, 25 Symbols of St Mark (*above*) and St Luke, from the Book of Durrow (Dublin, Trinity College, A.4.5.(57), ff. 21v and 191v)

between Pictish work and the Book of Durrow, a connection which will be seen continuously in the period up to *c*.800 (see below, pp. 114–19).

Is the Book of Durrow, then, of Northumbrian origin as the palaeographers seem to agree? A. A. Luce is the greatest protagonist of an Irish origin for the book. His arguments in the companion volume to the great facsimile edition published in 1960 are at once cogent and at times winsome, but he does point out that the Northumbrian provenance is entirely *a priori*:

> it is not based on the history or contents of the manuscript; it is not based on the palaeography of its script or on the art of its ornament; it has no basis in fact; it does not wear the look of truth. For some minds it has a quasi-basis in prejudice and a mistaken statement by Dr Lowe; but historically and in fact it is an *a priori* deduction from the Northumbrian theory of Irish art . . .

This is stirring stuff, but a quarter of a century later matters do not appear so clear cut and fine drawn. Luce's date of 625–50 can in no way be acceptable on the grounds of the hand, the ornament, the text or the general typology of the manuscript. The palaeographical judgement that it is Northumbrian seems firm. Nordenfalk says that the text possibly reflects 'the import of good Italian texts into Northumbria by Benedict Biscop', while in the totality of the art I can only agree with Bruce-Mitford and say that, although there are elements of Celtic art in the manuscript, the only likely place for its production is Northumbria and possibly again Lindisfarne, which had strong Irish and Scottish connections at this period (i.e. *c*.675). It is easy to hide behind the label Hiberno-Saxon for such art, but whilst that might be wise I feel that one should take the risk and call the Book of Durrow Northumbrian. So far as the art is concerned no element – other than the purely iconographical – had not occurred in England earlier.

The Lindisfarne school of manuscripts

The history of English art in the late seventh century is largely the history of manuscript illumination and we must turn next to the greatest of all English manuscripts, the Lindisfarne Gospels. Jewel-like, mind-teasing and eclectic, its ornament is a monument to the ability of the English artist, rather as the Rolls-Royce is a monument to British industry. The Lindisfarne Gospels (British Library, Cotton Nero D.iv) consists of 258 folios and measures 34 × 24 cm. It has five carpet pages (there may have been a sixth) and five pages bearing great initials. Further elaborate but smaller ornamental initials begin the prefaces, lists of chapters, lists of festivals and so on, and there are a number of other slightly enlarged initials scattered throughout the book. Each Gospel is preceded by an Evangelist portrait and at the beginning of the book there are sixteen pages of canon tables set in decorated arcading. The script, to quote Lowe, 'is a handsome and graceful Anglo-Saxon majuscule – one of the noblest examples of insular calligraphy by an English pen'. The paint on the ornamented pages is applied as a single layer and the layout of the design is composed (as we shall see) with great intricacy by means of compass and ruler. The tenth-century colophon (p. 13) gives us a traditional date for the manuscript between the death of St Cuthbert in 687 and the death of Eadfrith in 721 and, although a number of scholars have tried to date it to the end of this period, consensus follows Julian Brown and Rupert Bruce-Mitford in dating it immediately prior to the translation of St Cuthbert's relics in 698, although this date is by no means universally accepted. Brown and Bruce-Mitford have argued convincingly that Eadfrith not only wrote the text but illuminated its pages; if so, this is the first English work of art attributed to a known historical person.

It has been suggested that two other manuscripts from the Lindisfarne *scriptorium* survive, the Durham Gospels (Durham, Cathedral Library, A.II.17, ff. 2–102) and the Echternach Gospels (Paris, Bibliothèque Nationale, lat.9389). Less grand than the Lindisfarne Gospels, they are none the less splendid and striking works of art. The Durham manuscript might, indeed, have been nearly as rich and splendid as Lindisfarne, but much of the illuminated matter is missing. There were almost certainly Evangelist portraits, carpet pages and so on. What principally survives is the major group of initials at the beginning of St John's Gospel and a full-page depiction of the Crucifixion (the first such to survive in English art). It has a slightly larger page size (34 × 26 cm) than Lindisfarne but the difference is slight, as is the difference in size between Lindisfarne and Echternach (33.5 × 25.5 cm). Echternach is decorated with full-page miniatures and Evangelist symbols,

26 Initial from St John's Gospel, the Durham Gospels (Durham, Cathedral Library, A.II.17, fol. 69r)

27 *Opposite*: Crucifixion from the Durham Gospels (Durham, Cathedral Library, A.II.17, fol. 38v). 34 × 26 cm

26
27

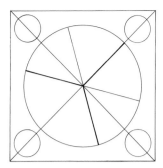

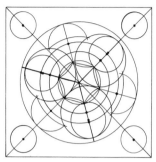

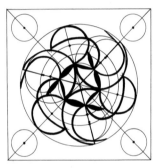

28 The construction of a spiral pattern on a carpet page of the Lindisfarne Gospels. See pl. 30

29 *Opposite*: enlarged detail from the Lindisfarne Gospels (London, British Library, Cotton Nero D.iv, fol. 94r). On the reverse of the carpet page preceding St Mark's Gospel the lines of construction of one of the roundels are clearly seen

canon tables and initials. The frames of the canon tables and symbols are much simpler than those of Lindisfarne, being executed mainly in plain orange and red. The St Matthew symbol is framed rather more elaborately with interlace ornament which (as in the Book of Durrow) subtly changes colour to tease the eye, although the design is in fact logical and symmetrical. There is no interlacing ornament in this book.

The ornament of the Durham Gospels is more elaborate than that of Echternach, closer perhaps to Lindisfarne, whilst Echternach appears to have been written and illuminated with some speed and consequent verve (consider the spontaneity for example of the symbol of St Mark). Durham has a rather more ponderous quality which only picks up spontaneity in the smaller initials in the text which are much more alive than the ornament of the rest of the manuscript and even of the comparable initials in the Lindisfarne Gospels. There is little reason to imagine that the same scribe was responsible for the three manuscripts (although Julian Brown and Rupert Bruce-Mitford are persuaded that Durham and Echternach are by the same hand), but most palaeographers would insist that all three were produced at Lindisfarne, perhaps at roughly the same time.

As representative of the art of the Lindisfarne school at its most splendid let us examine in some detail one of the carpet pages of the Lindisfarne Gospels (folio 94). Here is seen the true virtuosity of the artist and also the influences which went into his art. The frame consists of an outer element made up of birds and animals, the heads of which are in the middle of each side, the hind-quarters at the corners and the body forming the frame itself. Inside the frame are eleven dominating panels framed, as is the whole page, by bright orange-red borders, separated by blue and yellow with a touch of purple and a slight addition of orange to draw the eye to the centre of the page. In the centre is a circular panel with step patterns derived from cloisonné enamel or garnet work; similar motifs are seen in the side panels and between the square panels at top and bottom. These square panels contain trumpet-spiral patterns, while the remaining panels contain interlacing animals or interlacing animals and birds together. The whole pattern was carefully worked out before it was painted; lines of construction were drawn up and points of construction pricked out so that the page is carefully disciplined and not a single line or detail of the ornament is misplaced or destroys the balance of the whole design. Rupert Bruce-Mitford, who has analysed the ornament in great detail, has drawn attention to the method of construction of the central element of this page. The intersections of the design were drawn in dry point on the reverse of the page with compass and ruler and the main lines of construction pricked through to the ornamented face and then, by careful use of colour and emphasized line, the rectilinear step-pattern was built up. The whole of this page and all the other carpet pages were laid out in this fashion, as was much of the other ornament, and this is why there is a lack of spontaneity in the perfection of this manuscript.

Certain details of construction remain unresolved. The hair spirals, for example, which are such an important element in the manuscript art of the seventh and early eighth century cannot be drawn in any other manner than by free-hand. And yet it would be seemingly impossible to draw them free-hand with the pens then available unless the scribe either turned the paper, so that the thickness of line produced by the pen did not change, or used an instrument

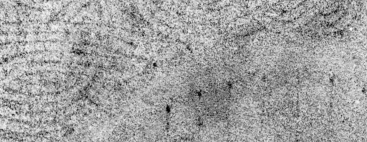

for appling the ink of which we have no surviving record and which was of a sophistication equal to that of the most modern draughtsman's drawing instrument. The artist of these three manuscripts in particular was obsessive in his attention to detail. If the fine scripts of the three manuscripts with their free flow and high legibility did not accompany the ornament one might compare it with such works of supererogation as writing the Lord's Prayer on postage stamps. And yet the effect is rich and, if obsessive, gorgeous; the master's intention was to tease the eye and draw the reader's attention into the page and hence to the text of the Gospels through a natural curiosity for intricacy. The fluency of line and the originality of the artist are clear; his intentions, particularly those of Eadfrith in the Lindisfarne Gospels, are not, although one might assume that they included an element of Christian duty and worship.

The intricacy of line and the motifs found in the Lindisfarne Gospels are all paralleled to a greater or lesser extent in what has gone before. Only the introduction of interlaced birds of a particular form is new. All are understandable, however, in the existing Anglo-Saxon–Irish–Scottish background; the script has strong Irish influences. One element which is entirely new and which is not repeated in this form for many years to come is the representations of the Evangelists. These are, for their period, highly naturalistic; only in sculpture is such naturalism found so early in Anglo-Saxon England. The Evangelist figures are based on Late Antique prototypes imported from the Mediterranean. Each Evangelist appears seated in three-quarter profile accompanied by his symbol; he is haloed and clothed in long flowing robes, his feet are bare but lines upon them perhaps reflect the Mediterranean sandals of the prototype (a form of footware probably unfamiliar to Anglo-Saxons from the cold north). The symbols are placed above the head (as though representing inspiration), each holds a book and for clarity is labelled (*imago leonis* – symbol of the lion for St Mark, for example). Each Evangelist is identified by his name preceded by the Greek words for 'the holy' (*O agios*) in Roman script. The representation of St Matthew is unusual in that it is accompanied by a bearded and haloed figure (perhaps Christ) peering from behind a curtain. There is some attempt at perspective in the drawing of the stools on which the figures sit, but it is not particularly successful (indeed in the case of St John the construction of the stool is completely misunderstood). The Evangelists are set against a pink background, but otherwise the palette used in their depiction is based on the colours found elsewhere in the book.

Bruce-Mitford has argued that the St Matthew portrait, long recognized as similar to the Ezra portrait in the Codex Amiatinus (see below, p. 49), was based on a Cassiodoran miniature of sixth-century date which was in Northumbria at the time, and that the other three Evangelists came from a Cassiodoran Gospel Book, perhaps the seventh volume seen in the cupboard behind Ezra in the Amiatinus manuscript. But the presence of a trumpet held by two of the Evangelist symbols has led David Wright to speculate that the source for at least two of the symbols may have been an Apocalypse.

The comparative dates of Durham, Echternach and Lindisfarne and the fragmentary, but closely allied, Northumbrian manuscript Corpus Christi College, Cambridge, 197B (with its badly burned British Library fragments, Cotton Otho C.v, which contains a lion very like the Evangelist symbol of Echternach) have been much discussed. Julian Brown has made a bold attempt

38
39

30 *Opposite*: carpet page from the Lindisfarne Gospels (London, British Library, Cotton Nero D.iv). 34 × 24 cm. See p. 38

31 David, from
Cassiodorus's *Commentary
on the Psalms*
(Durham, Cathedral
Library, B.II.30, fol. 81v).
See p. 61
32 Portrait and symbol of
St Luke, from the Lichfield
(or St Chad) Gospels, p.218
(Lichfield, Cathedral
Library). *c*.31 × 23.5 cm.
See p. 87

f. salur archan p cimulch. indra. p. iudnerch. Declencis f. Nobis epr copur teili
guid racendor teilian. dubnimo. et uhelin fili epr. sarnbri cam ibian. et fulgen
ac; qk fidele rcuppir. q cuftodienr li decner librarq; bleidiud 7plip rt
q h n cuftodienr. sit maledic; a do et a ruilian inct euangelio fcrip et
ur plr fnt fiat

33 Silver-gilt linked pins found in the River Witham at Fiskerton, Lincolnshire.
The technique used here is 'chip-carving', a term which derives from woodworking; by using the corner of a chisel at an angle an inverted pyramidal hole is made in the surface of the metal giving it facets which reflect the light at different angles. Length of central pin 11.5 cm. (London, British Museum)

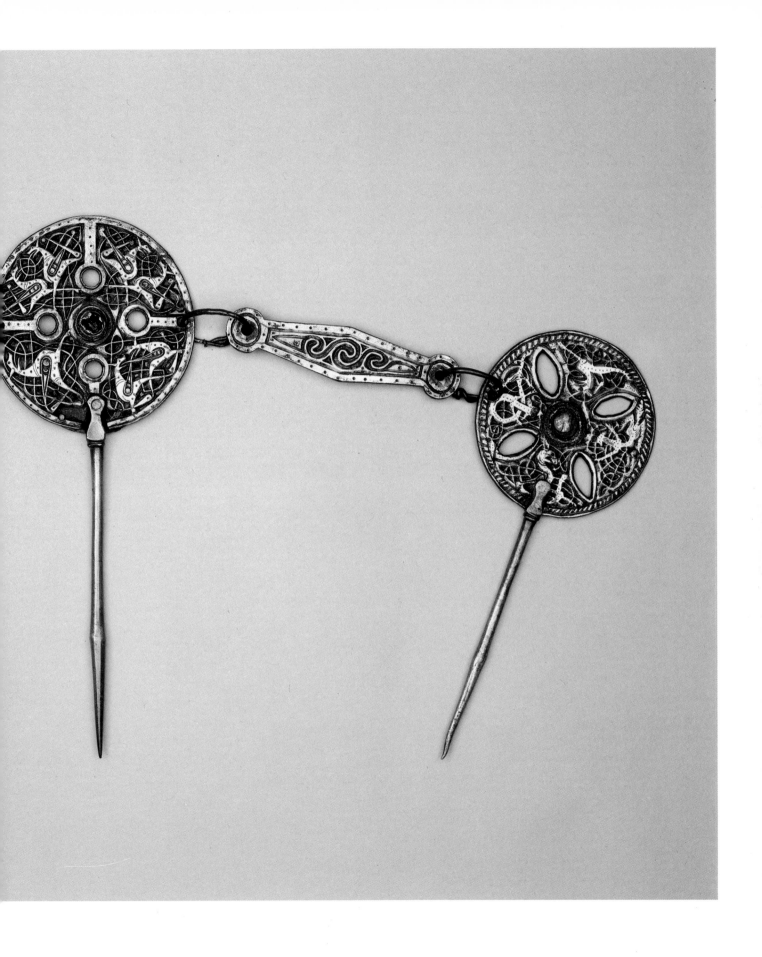

34–7 Four panels from the Franks Casket.
Above: Egil the Archer defending his home; *below*: the
story of Romulus and Remus; *opposite, above*: the Sack
of Jerusalem by the Emperor Titus; *opposite, below*: a
scene from the story of Weland the Smith, and the
Adoration of the Magi. Length of casket 23 cm.
(London, British Museum)

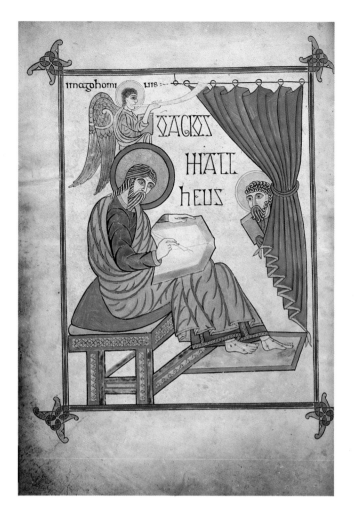

38 Portrait and symbol of St Matthew,
from the Lindisfarne Gospels
(London, British Library, Cotton Nero
D.iv, fol. 25v). 34 × 26 cm. See p. 40

39 Ezra, from the Codex Amiatinus
(Florence, Biblioteca Medicea
Laurenziana, Amiatinus I, fol. Vr).
50 × 34 cm. See p. 49

to place Durham, Echternach and Lindisfarne in sequence on the grounds of both palaeography and style, and eventually comes to the conclusion that Durham and Echternach were written by the same man, a contemporary of Eadfrith, the Lindisfarne Gospels scribe. This implies, if one believes that Lindisfarne was written for the translation of St Cuthbert, that all three manuscripts were completed within ten years of 700. The Corpus Christi College MS. 197B must belong to the same period, but perhaps to another *scriptorium*.

Manuscripts from Monkwearmouth and Jarrow

If Echternach, Durham and Lindisfarne have many insular traits in their ornamental make-up, the same cannot be said of the Codex Amiatinus (Florence, Biblioteca Medicea Laurenziana, Amiatinus I), one of the grandest of Anglo-Saxon manuscripts. It is big, comprising 1,030 folios and measuring 50 × 34 cm, and was one of three similar great books written in the twin monasteries of Monkwearmouth/Jarrow (fragments of one of the other manuscripts – unornamented – are preserved in the British Library, Add. 37777, 5025 and one sheet on loan). The Codex Amiatinus was being taken to Rome by Ceolfrid, the abbot of Monkwearmouth/Jarrow, when he died at Langres on 25 September 716. Rupert Bruce-Mitford and Per-Jonas Nordhagen have argued that it was written rather earlier than 716 – perhaps in the 690s; suffice it to say that it must have been written within a generation of the Lindisfarne group although I, for no real reason other than a feeling that it is stylistically later than Lindisfarne, would prefer a date nearer to 716 than 698. The text is the Vulgate version of St Jerome and was copied from a now lost book, the Codex Grandior of Cassiodorus, which Ceolfrid himself had brought back from Rome in 678.

The ornament consists of the frame of the dedicatory inscription, a portrait of Ezra, a full-page miniature of Christ in Majesty, the frames of the canon tables, a plan of the Temple at Jerusalem, various diagrams, a single relatively minor initial and one or two other flourishes. The representations of Christ and of Ezra are painted in an Italo-Byzantine style, which has a highly sophisticated treatment of three-dimensional form by the use of light and shade in an illusionistic manner. The Codex Amiatinus represents an attempt to introduce a pure Mediterranean style into Anglo-Saxon England, along with a Mediterranean purity of text. This attempt failed, for not until the tenth century was there any really successful introduction of Mediterranean styles into English manuscript ornament – and then at second hand. Ceolfrid failed and Eadfrith succeeded; the style which was to influence the English copyists of the next century was that so admirably exemplified in the Lindisfarne group of Gospel books. The Codex Amiatinus was perhaps too advanced in its stylistic approach to appeal to the taste of the English Church; its style never caught on.

The coffin of St Cuthbert and the first stone sculpture

One major monument of the end of the seventh century which relates to the manuscripts is the oak coffin-reliquary made for the translation of the body of St Cuthbert. The lid of the coffin is decorated with a full-length fieure of Christ, above and below which are Evangelist symbols. Each symbol is haloed and labelled in Roman or runic lettering. Michael and Gabriel appear on one end, the Virgin and Child on the other, the twelve Apostles on one side and five

39

44

42

43

49

40 Silver plate enshrining a wooden altar from the coffin of St Cuthbert, Durham Cathedral. Height 12.5 cm. (Durham, Cathedral Treasury)

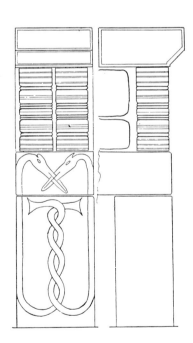

41 Soffit and front elevation of a jamb of the west doorway of St Peter, Monkwearmouth, Co. Durham

archangels on the other. The coffin is fragmentary and the style at first sight seems crude; after the sophistication of the contemporary manuscripts no amount of special pleading can persuade one that this is great art. Nevertheless, stylistically the figures are not without interest in that they relate clearly to the Lindisfarne Gospels. Haloed symbols and the use of lettering reflect the more sophisticated design of the Evangelist pages in the Gospels and remind us that much of the art of this period must have been carried out, in no great style, in wood.

Another object from the coffin may date from the translation of 698 – the enshrined portable altar. The original silver casing is fragmentary but on one face was a seated figure of St Peter, haloed and flanked by letters spelling out his name S[CS] P[ET]ROS A[POSTOLO]S. So much of this side is missing (for instance all the letters in square brackets) that I refrain from illustrating it in its normally reconstructed line-drawing, but it is mentioned here in that it obviously relates again to the seated figures in the Lindisfarne Gospels (if only for the inscription which is seen on either side of the body of the saint). The reverse of the altar (which has a later roundel in the centre) bears foliate designs and a linear cross.

40

The tiny glimpse provided of wooden sculpture by St Cuthbert's coffin-reliquary may or may not be typical of the wooden sculpture, both secular and lay, which has perished since the Anglo-Saxon period. What this sculpture looked like we do not know; but that it existed is certain, for references to wooden sculpture occur in contemporary literature. Buildings generally were of wood; dressed stone buildings were almost certainly first introduced by the Church, as was stone sculpture. At first this occurred only in the most sophisticated monasteries – Monkwearmouth, Jarrow, Lindisfarne, Ripon, Hexham and Canterbury, for example – and only later is it found in non-monastic churches in any quantity. The earliest surviving sculpture seems to comprise architectural fragments, furniture, string courses and other embellishing features of churches. Some of these – baluster shafts, for example – do not concern us here: we shall only deal with ornamented stones which are not merely in themselves architectural detail. The earliest datable piece of sculpture consists of a stone panel in each of the reveals of the main arch of the porticus at Monkwearmouth (founded 674 but probably completed c.685). The ornament on the panel consists of two intertwined snakes, set symmetrically with interlocking jaws, clearly related to the animal ornament of the Book of Durrow and with a long Anglo-Saxon tradition behind it. The flat appearance of the carving might suggest a wooden model, which is hardly typical of the sculptural tradition which was to follow. The Monkwearmouth slab seems to have few parallels apart from an unstratified slab (no. 9) from Monkwearmouth and possibly the frame of a sundial from the nearby church of Escomb.

41

More innovatory was semi-naturalistic animal sculpture in the round, examples of which are seen at Monkwearmouth and Hexham. At the latter site, imposts bearing a lion and a boar are perhaps to be associated with Bishop Wilfrid's great church (founded 673–4). The stones bear traces of paint (it should be borne in mind that much of the sculpture which now appears so bland in churches and churchyards throughout the country was originally highly coloured – mostly in black and red). The Hexham animals form part of a frieze, the origins of which may perhaps be seen in similar features on the

45, 46

42–4 The wooden coffin reliquary of St Cuthbert, probably made for the translation of his body in 698.
Far left: drawing of the lid, with Christ and symbols of the Evangelists.
Above: end, with the Virgin and Child.
Left: view of the whole coffin, as reconstructed from fragments. Reconstructed length of coffin 1.69 m. (Durham, Cathedral Treasury)

45–7 Fragments of sculpture at Hexham,
Northumberland.
Above: Anglo-Saxon imposts: *left*, a lion (length 29 cm);
right, a boar (length 31.4 cm). *Below*: Romano-British
vine-scroll ornament. Height 30.5 cm

early Christian churches of the Near East, whence the idea may well have been transmitted by way of Italy. As, however, the stones are not in their original context we must be careful how we date them.

Thus we face the major problem of Anglo-Saxon sculpture: it is clear that very little of it can be dated. No surviving piece of sculpture is dated by primary inscription (excluding dedication stones, which are in any case unornamented); however, a very few pieces (the Monkwearmouth slab is one of the few) are dated because they belong to the original fabric of a church of known date. Otherwise dating depends on less reliable criteria: the discovery of sculpture in sealed archaeological levels (as at York, Jarrow, Cambridge and Deerhurst, Gloucestershire); the presence of sculptured stones used as building materials in rebuilt (late) churches (as at Middleton and Kirkdale in Yorkshire); on stylistic dating of the ornament by cross-dating to objects (like manuscripts) of known date; or on the linguistic dating (no more refined than stylistic dating) of inscriptions which appear on the stones.

177

It is, consequently, difficult to date any piece of pre-tenth-century sculpture with any degree of certainty. Thus we may postulate that the Hexham sculpture belongs to Wilfrid's church only because it has a sub-classical naturalism possibly inimical to an Anglo-Saxon mind and unlike the later (eighth-century) sculpture about which, stylistically, a great deal more is known. The difficulty of dating and identification is well illustrated by a number of pieces of Hexham sculpture which have at various times been taken as Anglo-Saxon but which have been convincingly argued to be Romano-British, most recently by Rosemary Cramp: these include two fragments of vine-scroll ornament and a panel containing a rosette. There is much re-used Roman masonry in the Anglo-Saxon churches of Northumbria and it is hardly surprising to find Roman ornamental panels built into later church walls. Such finds perhaps indicate a possible origin for some of the sculptural motifs found in Anglo-Saxon contexts: with the reintroduction into England, for the first time since the Roman period, of stone buildings of substance and sophistication, the Anglo-Saxons may well have turned to the visible remains of the earlier period, not only for building material but also for ornamental inspiration. Few standing Romano-British buildings were actually re-used by the Anglo-Saxons (although it is probable, for example, that part of the Roman forum at York served the newly converted as a Christian church), but the Anglo-Saxons were very conscious of their presence, as can be seen from the literature. Stone was often transported from distant Roman buildings, as at Escomb, Co. Durham, or – as at Reculver, Kent – re-used on site. The possibility, therefore, of Romano-British standing monuments influencing the art of this country cannot be dismissed. Although we know that continental masons were introduced into northern England in the seventh century and, although it was to Monkwearmouth/Jarrow that the Pictish king Nechtan wrote in 716 for instruction in building 'in the Roman manner', there is no written evidence concerning the source of the English sculptural tradition. We have seen that one of the traditions to which the stone sculptor turned at Monkwearmouth was not Gaulish, Mediterranean or Romano-British, but English.

47

Herein lies the chronological difficulty. There seems a great reluctance among students of Anglo-Saxon sculpture to date any sculpture to the seventh century other than some few architectural fragments from Hexham,

Monkwearmouth and Jarrow. Accepting the fact that there was a highly sophisticated building tradition by the late seventh century, they see stone sculpture (as far as the free-standing cross is concerned) as no earlier than the eighth century. What then is the difference between the free-standing and the fixed? It can, of course, be said that no Germanic-derived ornament appears on free-standing sculpture (it is rare enough in any case) and that the type of motif depicted on the crosses and other monuments – the vine-scroll, iconographic representation of the Christian story and certain more abstract patterns – are typologically or even stylistically later introductions into the content of the art, as is shown, for example, by the fact that they never occur in the well-dated early manuscripts. This is the strongest argument, but it has many holes. For example, the models for sculpture and manuscript ornament may well have been different (this is clearly so in the eighth century). Certain motifs in architectural sculpture (interlace ornament particularly, but also spiraliform designs) could be much earlier than is normally admitted. Indeed, the form of the free-standing stone cross could itself be earlier, especially as we have early references to such crosses in literature: the earliest being to the *wooden* cross erected by King Oswald in 633 after the battle of Heavenfield.

If more architectural sculpture occurred *in situ* it might be possible to date the sculpture more closely. Jarrow we have seen to be a well-dated church, but the small surviving eastern church is devoid of ornament and there is no record

48, 49 Two fragments showing plant-scrolls and inhabited plant-scrolls, from Jarrow

50 Fragment of a decorative frieze
from Jarrow, showing a portion of an
inhabited plant-scroll

of any *in situ* ornament in the larger western church destroyed in the early part of the nineteenth century. At Jarrow, however, were found architectural fragments decorated with plant-scrolls and inhabited vine-scrolls – even the figure of a hunter – which have details in common with ornament found on a much worn cross-shaft (Jarrow no. 2): if these sculptured fragments belonged to the basilica dedicated in 685, it would then be possible to say that at least one free-standing cross could be tentatively dated to the seventh century.

48, 49

50

For the moment we have to be content with a floating chronology. Whilst it is certain that some architectural sculpture can be dated to the seventh century, there is no evidence that any free-standing sculpture can be so dated. Even the stones tentatively associated with Wilfrid's church at Hexham cannot be definitely so identified. It seems wiser then to deal with all the earlier stone sculpture together in the next chapter, for it bears little relevance to the generality of seventh-century art, save in the case of the two happily datable slabs at Monkwearmouth. It should also be emphasized that there is in most scholars' view no evidence for any priority of sophisticated ornamental sculpture in Scotland or Ireland and that the influences cannot be said to come thence (see below, pp. 113ff.). All the evidence would suggest, as with the incised Pictish stones which may have received Anglo-Saxon influence in the seventh century, that the Scottish and Irish artists were recipients rather than donors at this period.

Metalwork

17, 40

Which leaves the problem of the metalwork. The St Cuthbert objects – the cross perhaps dating from the middle of the century and the altar possibly from 698 – have been the only two specifically Christian metal objects mentioned in this chapter. It should not, however, be overlooked that Sutton Hoo is dated to the seventh century and, as has been pointed out, there is a fair amount of metalwork of pagan Anglo-Saxon inspiration surviving from the Christian period. The year 700 is not a mystical date: it may be that, like the sculpture, some of the metalwork discussed as eighth century in the next chapter may have been made at the same time as the Book of Durrow or the Lindisfarne Gospels. What can be said, however, is that there is little to indicate a change in metalworking style until the very end of the seventh century when the altar of St Cuthbert brings vegetal ornament into the corpus. It is clear that the seventh century witnessed the end of a long metalworking tradition. Sutton Hoo provided the final flowering of a style which had its roots in the late Roman world. While not everything was lost in the succeeding centuries (witness the cell-like step pattern in the Lindisfarne Gospels), the jeweller took new directions. Enamelling and garnet work to all intents disappear, the animal style is converted into something different through contact with naturalism and with the inhabited plant-scroll (which latter will be examined in the next chapter). In sum, there is little of relevance to the further development of the metalworker's craft in the seventh-century English material. Strangely, the metalwork influences the manuscripts and, as far as we can tell from what little survives, not the later jewellery – a feature which we encounter again in the ninth century and one which might suggest the primacy of the jeweller as artist in this middle Anglo-Saxon period.

51

Apart from an unpublished piece with animal ornament from Bamburgh, Northumberland, one metal object deserves mention in this context, a piece of impressed silver from Hexham which is almost certainly of seventh-century date. The plaque portrays in naïve fashion the head and shoulders of a haloed cleric carrying a book and perhaps wearing a pallium (an episcopal vestment). In style it is closely related to the incised figures on the St Cuthbert reliquary-coffin. It is, however, unique but does at least show that objects decorated in this style were present in materials other than wood.

It will be remarked that practically no material discussed in this chapter was

51 Impressed silver plaque, with figure
of a haloed cleric. From Hexham,
Northumberland. 10.5 × 7 cm.
(London, British Museum)

made south of the Humber. Although the Church was well established in the
south, no monuments, illuminated manuscripts or specifically Christian
objects (other than a handful of pendant crosses) have survived to this day
which can be assigned to southern England. The reason for this is not clear; it
is presumably purely accidental. Remains of church buildings of this period
are known in the south and metalwork (in the pagan tradition) is common. It is
hard to believe that all the innovatory artistic endeavour of the Anglo-Saxons
in the century after the Conversion was concentrated in Northumbria; there
must have been some activity in the south. But of this we have, alas, no
evidence.

3 The eighth and ninth centuries

THE FRONTIERS OF NORTHUMBRIA, established in the seventh century, were to remain relatively unbroken until the second half of the ninth century when the whole of the North was taken over by Scandinavian settlers. The Northumbrian kings were reasonably strong and self-sufficient and although they indulged in occasional military adventures they managed to preserve their power and their identity. The Church continued to increase in power. Donations of money and estates added to the wealth and influence of such monasteries as Lindisfarne and Whitby. The archbishopric at York was an important political factor in Northumbria and the archbishop himself sometimes challenged the primacy of Canterbury. Learning was in the ascendency; the century which produced Bede at the beginning produced Alcuin at its end. Great libraries were established: Acca, bishop of Hexham from 710 to 781, built up a 'very large and very noble library', while the library of York was celebrated, almost catalogued, in verse by Alcuin. Books were sent to the missionaries on the Continent and other books were brought from Italy and from the many monasteries of France. The fame of English scholars spread and Bede's writings were distributed throughout northern Europe. Alcuin himself was attracted to the court of Charlemagne and went with honour from York to become abbot of Tours and also of the monasteries of St Lupus at Troyes and of Ferrières, all of which were to become great centres of learning and art. His scholarship is considered to have been conventional, but as a teacher his influence was dominant. His practical efficiency in teaching was to influence, through his pupils and colleagues, the totality of European learning for many generations.

As the Northumbrians consolidated their political, economic and cultural assets, so the Mercians developed theirs. When Bede completed his *Ecclesiastical history* in 731 he saw all the kingdoms south of the Humber as subject to Æthelbald, king of Mercia. This was a state of affairs which continued until the end of the century under the greatest of all Mercian kings, Offa. In style Offa's reign may be compared with Charlemagne's – indeed Charlemagne appears to have treated Offa as an equal: 'Charles, by the grace of God, king of the Franks and the Lombards, to his dearest brother, Offa, king of the Mercians'. There is no doubt about Offa's aggressive pursuit of power – by conquest of the southern and eastern kingdoms of England, by marriage alliances (one daughter married the king of Northumbria, the other the king of Wessex), by great military works like Offa's Dyke, by his encouragement of merchants, by his development of a standard coinage and by his support of the Church. The Mercian Church, like the Northumbrian, became richer and more powerful. Towards the end of his reign Offa even established an archdiocese (short lived it is true) at Lichfield. Some of the great monuments of Anglo-Saxon architecture – as for example the church at Brixworth – might belong to the century of Mercian supremacy.

52 *Opposite*: All Saints, Brixworth, Northamptonshire, from the south-west.
The main body of the church (the nave and lower portion of the tower) probably dates from the late eighth or early ninth century

59

When Offa died in July 796 the centralized control he had established over much of southern England began to disintegrate. Kent gradually became more independent, at first under the influence or subjection of Mercia and then under Wessex. But Kent had a great advantage: the importance of Canterbury and the archbishopric with which it was associated was immense, particularly in cultural terms. Gifts to the monasteries of Canterbury brought money into the kingdom and this, with the prestige of the archbishopric, made the small kingdom a desirable polity for strong kings. Kent also had one of the most important mints in England – again at Canterbury – and through its ports easy access to the rich markets of the Continent.

But the dominant southern kingdom in the ninth century was undoubtedly Wessex, which in the early years of the century increased vastly in power and wealth. Under Egbert not only was the south-east (including London) conquered, but in 829 Mercia and Essex were also brought under the control of Wessex, and Northumbria was laid waste. Egbert and his successors were never so powerfully stable as Offa. Mercia and London were lost and the attacks of the Scandinavians, particularly in the third quarter of the ninth century, reduced Wessex to a fortress, a role which was admirably developed by Alfred at the end of the century when he paved the way for English victory and for his successors' consolidation of the whole of England in the middle years of the tenth century. The cultural life of the country was nurtured by Alfred; but what actually happened in Wessex, artistically and culturally, in the years before Alfred's reign is difficult to interpret.

In reconstructing the history of ornament in the eighth and early ninth centuries we are presented with a chronological morass, much worse than the situation in the seventh century (where only the sculpture was problematic). There are practically no fixed points but there is a mass of material, much of it unprovenanced or of doubtful attribution. Geographically we can fix certain stylistic elements on the basis of the sculptural remains; chronologically there exist only one or two internally dated illuminated manuscripts, a few objects found in coin hoards (but nothing before *c.*850) and two or three objects which bear the names of known historical figures. Unfortunately few, if any, objects have been found in well-dated archaeological deposits, although one may hope that some of the ninth-century York material so laboriously excavated in the 1970s will ultimately be dated when tree-ring analyses of the various contexts in which the material was found have been worked out. Throughout this chapter we must remember that there is no absolute date for any ornamented object between the Leningrad Bede (*c.*746) and the Æthelwulf finger-ring (839–58).

Although the high point of early English Christian art was reached within a generation of 700, it was during the late seventh and eighth centuries that English art was at its most influential in two areas – in the Celtic north and west of Britain and in Gaul (what was to become the Carolingian Empire). The great art of the Northumbrian tradition provided inspiration, even models, for the art of the neighbouring countries. When the king of the Picts wanted to build stone churches he sent to Monkwearmouth/Jarrow for advice; when Charlemagne wanted a scholar he sent to York for Alcuin. With these contacts went the art, the traditions and perhaps even the artists.

The art of the non-Anglo-Saxon areas of the British Isles reached its apogee towards the end of the eighth century with the Book of Kells, which was

54, 55
117

60

perhaps a product of the great monastery at Iona (see below, p. 129), with the early Irish high crosses and with the metalwork, particularly the Ardagh Chalice (see below, p. 120) – dare we date it as early as 700? – and the Pictish treasure from St Ninian's Isle, Shetland (see below, p. 117). Carolingian art received its initial stimulus while Charlemagne was still king of the Franks (long before his coronation in 800) and produced, as well as some masterpieces of metalwork to which we shall return (p. 130ff.), two exceptional schools of manuscript painting – the Ada school (780 and later) and the Palace school (dated after 795). The Palace school was influenced from Byzantium, but the Ada school depended on Italian and particularly on English sources for its inspiration. English influence is seen in the great initials, lavish interlace patterns and smaller initials which encompass tiny religious scenes like those to be seen in eighth-century Anglo-Saxon manuscripts. It is not too much of an exaggeration to say that the Carolingian flowering of art depended in many respects on an Hiberno-Saxon tradition: a tradition which had taken Anglo-Saxon and Irish missionaries and scholars to Fulda and Bobbio, and which later brought Alcuin to the court of Charlemagne. The Merovingian art of the late seventh and early eighth centuries was poor stuff, provincial and soon ousted by influences – directly or indirectly transmitted – from England, Ireland and Italy.

While few surviving eighth- and ninth-century manuscripts anywhere hint at the sophistication and innovation achieved by the Northumbrian manuscripts of the late seventh and early eighth centuries, the influence of these later manuscripts was felt abroad and at home provided a rich source for inventiveness. At the same time the more public aspects of art, clearly seen in sculpture, reached heights of achievement not equalled for at least two centuries, and the art of the metalworker and ivory carver developed a new and lively tradition which was to interact continuously with the other media to produce objects sometimes as sophisticated as anything produced in the later medieval period.

The manuscript tradition

It is convenient to begin a survey of this period with the early eighth-century manuscripts which demonstrate continuing traditions from the Lindisfarne Gospel group. No southern English illumination survives, so the picture must be imbalanced; but three or four manuscripts demonstrate the continuing Northumbrian tradition. The manuscript which is most closely tied to this stylistic tradition is a copy – the earliest known – of Cassiodorus's *Commentary on the Psalms* (Durham, Cathedral Library, B.II.30), which may have been written at Monkwearmouth/Jarrow (although opinions concerning its original provenance differ). Traditionally associated with Bede it may indeed date from his time (or at least from within a few years of his death), say from the second quarter of the eighth century. This book forms a useful introduction to the subject because, although a book of the study or the pulpit, it is a grand manuscript of the same size as the Durham Gospels (A.II.17) and the Codex Amiatinus: it measures 42 × 29.5 cm. The 266 surviving folios include two full-page miniatures of David, one of which is a seated figure, rather incompetently drawn, with a small head plonked on a schematic, but well proportioned, robed body. The chair appears as a two-dimensional ladder-like frame with animal head terminals and the whole figure is

31

61

surrounded by rectangular panels containing interlaced ribbon and animal ornament. The colours include various shades of pink, green and orange and much of the ribbon interlace is reserved against a black background. Dotted circles appear as a background to the figure and there are flourishes of interlace at the corners of the frame. Whilst the interlace and animal ornament is executed in a reasonably competent style, there is a looseness about the whole composition which shows a departure from the tight discipline of the Lindisfarne and the Durham Gospels. Another full-page picture of David (in this case standing) has a less ornate frame, the ornament being confined to ribbon interlace and simple, if intricate, step motifs. Richard Bailey has shown that the interlace patterns were marked out in dry-point and were further planned by means of a series of pin holes. The nimbus and the circles around

53

the labels were produced by compass, the hole of the compass point being clearly visible. The dotted circles were produced in the same way. A number of enlarged initials with zoomorphic characteristics are scattered throughout the manuscript, the largest spanning seven lines.

Whilst the figure drawing is clearly derived from an Italian model, the interlace and animal ornament can undoubtedly be traced back to insular sources, providing but a pale reflection of the grandeur of the manuscripts we have considered in the last chapter. Suggestions have been made that the two pictures of David were by separate hands. I see no evidence for this; the palette is approximately the same (although more limited on the page with the standing figure) and the interlace in particular seems to chime on both pages. Related to this book is the Leningrad copy of Bede's *Ecclesiastical history* (Leningrad, Public Library, Cod. Q.v.I.18), the fourth hand of which is so closely related to the hand that glossed the Durham Cassiodorus that the two might even have been written by the same man. The Leningrad Bede is a Monkwearmouth/Jarrow manuscript, but the fourth scribe according to Lowe may have been trained elsewhere. We are thus no nearer a provenance for the great commentary on the Psalms, although York has been adumbrated as a source.

The Leningrad Bede has been dated on complicated internal evidence to 746 and this date seems to be accepted by palaeographers and historians alike. The modest illumination consists of two initial letters, a B and an H. Each introduces a new element into Anglo-Saxon art and, in the case of the H, into European art, for here we have the first known historiated initial (a letter adorned with figures). Within the hoop of the letter (itself decorated with very competent interlace) is a half-length figure of a saint which a later hand has identified within the halo as Augustine (although, as the sentence introduced by the initial refers to Gregory the Great, this is almost certainly a misidentification). The colours are, to use Alexander's words, 'unexpectedly bright . . . the halo and saint's underrobe being pale yellow, his cloak slate-blue and his book pinky-red'. The figure contains the same mixture of Italian and insular influence seen in the earlier manuscripts, but its proportions are more competent than the figures of the Durham Cassiodorus, perhaps more closely related to the Lindisfarne group. This is the first occasion on which a recognizable idea is represented by a drawing to illustrate the text. (Some scholars, Alexander and Wright for example, maintain, however, that the Vespasian Psalter, which is discussed below, is earlier. This, however, as we shall see, seems to be a nonsense.) Although used occasionally elsewhere in Anglo-Saxon art (and copied as we have noted by Carolingian artists) this form of pictorial narrative does not become widespread until the twelfth century.

The second initial is less startling, but also introduces a new element into manuscript art – a plant ornament. In the upper part of the letter B is a balanced vine-scroll, the terminal leaves on either side being of pointed form, the grapes represented (rather schematically) as bunches of three or in some cases like single cherries. The lower loop of the letter encloses a plant with a bud flanked by lobed, conjoined leaves. The plant-scroll is, however, probably more interesting as it appears to be the earliest – if not the only – accurately dated example of this motif from a Northumbrian source and typifies a design which extends in many forms into all media at this period.

54, 55 Two initials, H and B, from the Leningrad manuscript of Bede's *Ecclesiastical history* (Leningrad, Public Library, Cod. Q.v.I.18, ff. 3v, 26v)

56, 57 Plant-scrolls on the Ormside Bowl (see pl. 159)

58, 59 Ornament on the ends of the Gandersheim Casket (*opposite*)

The plant-scroll

The vine-scroll is a Christian motif with origins in Mediterranean and perhaps Near Eastern Christianity. It is reasonably certain that it represents Christ – 'I am the true vine' (John, xv, 1). It occurs in a great variety of forms, which are often hardly recognizable as vines – hence although the origin is reasonably clear, it is wiser to follow the practice of the *Corpus of Anglo-Saxon sculpture* and use the term 'plant-scroll'. There are two major varieties of scroll, which may have had separate origins in the Mediterranean, but which by the time they appear in Anglo-Saxon England seem to have been used alongside each other. The first was the plain plant-scroll, often finely represented with bunches of grapes, sometimes (as in the Leningrad Bede) in a less understandable form, as berries or as leaves. It occurs as a tree, as a balanced plant, as a scroll of undulating form with alternate bunches of grapes in the concave spaces, and as an irregular filler pattern within fields. The second form consists of the inhabited scroll, in which are caught up birds, animals, monsters and even men. These creatures can be completely naturalistic or degenerate until they become part of the scroll itself; only the head, perhaps, being recognizable. Sometimes late in the eighth century animals also appear by themselves with vegetal tails or bodies, presumably deriving from the plant-scroll but now out of context. With the addition of the plant-scroll in its various forms and with the lobed frond the ornamental repertoire of eighth- and ninth-century Anglo-Saxon art is completed.

An interesting and rich example of the inhabited plant-scroll is that which appears in embossed silver on the exterior of the Ormside Bowl, an elaborate object found in the churchyard of that name in Westmorland. The bowl is little more than a cup, measuring only 13.3 cm in diameter at its mouth. The plant-scroll on the bowl terminates in a number of different forms from full bunches of grapes to leaves or (as in the Leningrad Bede) cherry-like fruit with or without a median leaf. The vine is inhabited by a variety of creatures which range from the naturalistic to the grotesque. Collared birds of naturalistic form eat the grapes and various animals, none of them identifiable as a particular species and some of which verge on the grotesque, display themselves in the scrolls. There are enough parallels between the plant ornament of the Ormside Bowl and the Leningrad Bede to date the bowl tentatively to the first half of the eighth century, although it was renovated later.

Although the plant-scroll appears in innumerable forms in stone sculpture (to which we shall return) it might be useful – as so much of the stonework is in bad condition and difficult to photograph – to look at the degeneration of the

159

56, 57

60 The Gandersheim Casket. 12.6 × 12.6 × 6.8 cm. (Herzog Anton Ulrich Museum, Brunswick)

motif in metalwork and the related craft of ivory and bone carving. There are purer examples of the inhabited plant-scroll in the sculpture, but some of the first elements of degeneration are clearly seen on the gable end of the Gandersheim Casket (sometimes known as the Brunswick Casket). This bronze-mounted, bone object has sometimes been falsely associated with the Abbey of Ely by a runic inscription on the base, which has been shown to be modern (whether copying an old original or not is uncertain); even if it were genuine the identity of Ely in the inscription is doubtful. The rest of the casket is ancient, and stylistically it must belong to the middle or late eighth century. The plant-scroll of the casket has highly formalized berries and leaves and the scrolls produce the forequarters and head of animals. On the main faces the plant-scrolls have disappeared and the animals' bodies interlace with each other in regular apposition, in a manner not unlike that which occurs in balanced plant compositions.

60

58, 59

65

61 Ivory plaque, possibly from a casket. 13.2 × 8.1 cm. (London, Victoria and Albert Museum)

66

62 Runic-inscribed mount from the River Thames, near Westminster Bridge, London.
Length 18.8 cm. (London, British Museum)

A mixture of interlaced animals and vine-scroll is also to be seen on an ivory plaque, also possibly from a casket, in the Victoria and Albert Museum, London (some see it as a continental object of Anglo-Saxon inspiration). This displays an intermediate stage between the almost completely degenerate inhabited scroll of the Gandersheim Casket and the rather more naturalistic scroll of the Ormside Bowl. Two almost square panels are decorated with animals and birds caught up in interlaced ribbon – which does not, as in the case of the Gandersheim examples, grow out of their tails. In the border is a true inhabited scroll containing birds and animals. The scroll produces bunches of grapes, fronds and trefoil leaf groups. It is interesting however that in this scroll we see the degeneration apparent in the Gandersheim Casket, perhaps even in a rather advanced form, for in the bottom corners each scroll terminates in an animal head with a protruding tongue. This process reaches a *reductio ad absurdum* in chip-carved gilt bronze and silver, where the animal head is all that is left of the inhabited plant-scroll, the rest of the ornament being merely ribbon interlace of a very simple form. This can be seen (but is not illustrated) on the binding strips of the Gandersheim Casket.

The circular heads of the three conjoined silver-gilt pins found in the River Witham at Fiskerton, Lincolnshire, demonstrate the various stages in this degeneration. Two of the pin-heads bear fine expressions of eighth-century animal ornament executed in chip-carving; the central pin in particular has splendidly formed winged bipeds caught up in interlace. Their bodies are decorated with a dotted ornament and they have elongated wings ending in a slight lobe. This is the best animal ornament in metalwork of the middle of the eighth century. The style was probably based regionally in middle England from southern Mercia into southern Northumbria. The point to be made in this context, however, is that on the left-hand pin only one animal can be seen; the other three panels are filled with ribbon interlace with occasional vegetal terminals, an element which looks like the pot from the 'potted plant' type of scroll together with elongated wings. (It should be said that this pin-head is of such a different style from its companion pieces that it may be a replacement.)

What is perhaps a more northerly version of the process seen on the Witham Pins occurs on the startling new find of a helmet from York. The nose-guard of the object is decorated with animals which have a slight foliate element in the treatment of the crests which spring from their heads and whose bodies degenerate into interlace ornament. The treatment of the animal heads is very close to the head which terminates a Northumbrian, runic-inscribed mount from the River Thames at London, and indeed the ribbing and plastic treatment of the animal head and eyebrow ridges of the helmet add to the similarities. The ridge of the helmet has an inscription in Latin, signed with an Old English name (Oshere): IN NOMINE.DNI.NOSTRI.IHU.SPS.D(?)EI. OMNIBUS.AMEN.OSHERE.XPI (In the name of our Lord Jesus, [the Holy] Spirit, God [the Father], all [the Saints]. Amen. Oshere. Christ). The object is difficult to date, but the early eighth century is not impossible.

61

33

63, 64

62

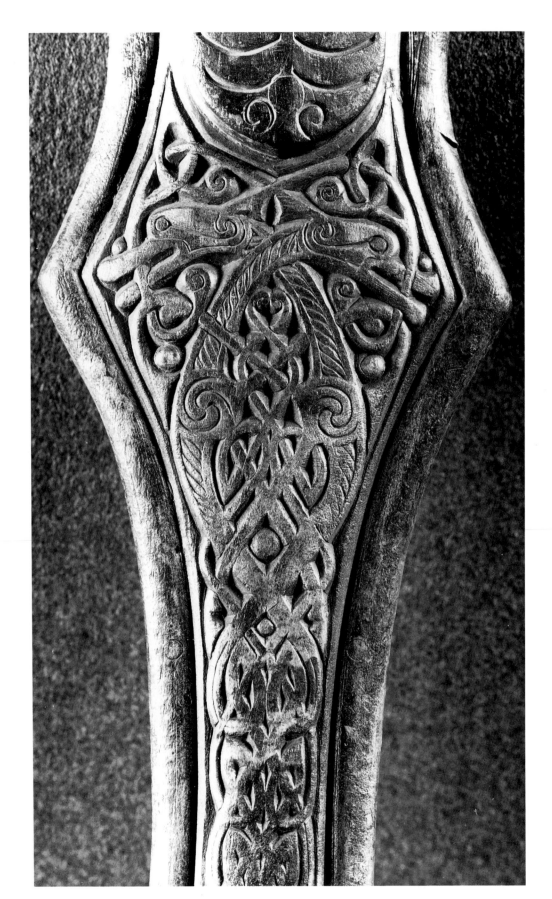

63, 64 Helmet found at Coppergate, York, and (*right*) detail of the nose-guard.
Height of helmet 31.2 cm.
(York, Castle Museum)

65–8 Four of the stone fragments from Reculver, Kent. Heights between 30 and 35 cm. (Canterbury Cathedral)

Stone sculpture – memorials and architectural detail

We shall return to small objects of ivory, bone and metal, but let us turn now to stone sculpture of the eighth century. Much of the stone carving mentioned so far comprises architectural detail or church furnishing. Another type of sculpture has yet to be considered, namely funerary monuments. The standing cross is the commonest form, but other monuments – grave covers in various house-shaped or coped forms, memorial crosses, simple non-cruciform grave-markers and so on – are known. Other sculptured free-standing monuments in the form of crosses or pillars also occur. These are not memorial stones but function as boundary or sanctuary markers, preaching crosses or pious reminders of the Christian message. Such outstanding monuments as the

69–71
72–4

Ruthwell and Bewcastle crosses may well have been objects of worship, but of this we have no direct evidence. Sculpture is, however, occasionally mentioned in more or less contemporary literature. The cross set up by St Cuthbert on Farne before his death in 687 could well have been carved with ornamental motifs or scenes of Christian propaganda, but whether this cross was of stone or wood is not known; the cross (mentioned above) set up at Heavenfield by St Oswald after 633 was certainly of wood. A decorated stone cross was, according to Symeon of Durham (a late source), erected in memory of Acca at

76

Hexham after his death in 740. Indeed one of the Hexham crosses has often been identified as this memorial stone (without much justification).

Having little if any absolute chronology for free-standing stone sculptures we can only turn to stylistic or typological methods of dating. Frankly these are unsatisfactory for very many reasons. First, stone sculpture differs greatly in quality: the grand pieces – the Ruthwell and Bewcastle crosses, for example – are of an entirely different quality from that of much of the minor sculpture and perhaps too much attention is paid to them and not enough to minor pieces. Second, the crosses have hitherto been badly recorded. The British Academy *Corpus of Anglo-Saxon sculpture*, the first volume of which appeared in 1984 (after Herculean work on the part of Rosemary Cramp), will

70

eventually describe and illustrate all the Anglo-Saxon sculpture in England; but for the moment we rely largely on local surveys (like those of Collingwood for Yorkshire and Calverley for Cumbria) which, while magnificent in their time, are now long out-dated (some more than seventy years old) and poorly illustrated. Other surveys have merely been summaries of the state of the study at a given time. Third, although much work has been done on the descriptive grammar of sculptural ornament, few people have been willing to admit to bafflement in arranging the disparate motifs (of varying quality) in a chronological sequence. And this is particularly true of the period up to say 950. If I admit that I am often baffled by chronological and stylistic considerations in relation to most pre-tenth-century Anglo-Saxon sculpture, it might be said that I have no business to write – or attempt to write – this book. But this is the situation and I believe that many specialists in Anglo-Saxon art are similarly affected, although few admit it.

As an extreme example take the famous fragments of stone from Reculver, 65–8 Kent, widely acclaimed as the most remarkable and innovatory group of Anglo-Saxon sculpture in insular art. The latest Ph.D. thesis on the subject dates them to the seventh century (and even perhaps to the early seventh century), whilst Kendrick, following their original publisher, placed the group in the late seventh century, 'to the early days of the Kentish renaissance'. Rosemary Cramp would now, I think, date them to the eighth century. Dominic Tweddle, who is the most recent scholar to analyse the Reculver sculptures, places them in the ninth century by comparison with the Canterbury Bible (below, p. 94), the St Cuthbert stole and the Corpus Christi 103, 192 *Life of St Cuthbert*. He has pointed to what he considers Carolingian 193, 203 classicizing trends, which are also to be seen on a number of architectural capitals from St Augustine's Abbey, Canterbury, in an effort to support this date. His analysis is carefully argued but not altogether convincing, although many of his arguments are worth consideration. Talbot Rice, however, who was often wayward in his discussion of English art, dated it firmly and with

69–71 The Ruthwell Cross.
Above: Christ as Judge, trampling
upon a lion and an adder. *Opposite*:
(*left*) Mary Magdalene washing
Christ's feet, with the Annunciation
below; (*right*) inhabited plant-scrolls.
(Parish church of Ruthwell, Dumfries)

some reason to the tenth century on the basis of the style of the drapery. His arguments, indeed, seem cogent when one considers the almost total lack of Anglo-Saxon sculpture of the early period in the south-east. On balance, however, the sculpture should perhaps be dated to the eighth century (and quite late in that century). Talbot Rice's interpretation of the drapery is over-optimistic and the form which the sculpture took – a round shaft – would certainly fit more easily within the late eighth-century series (although the Wolverhampton Pillar, p. 105, is dated later). It does, however, present a major iconographical problem – and, what is more, a problem of iconographical transmission – which has not yet been solved. The sculpture is also *sui generis* in that it is unique in its area. The dating of Anglo-Saxon sculpture is surrounded by pitfalls.

Ruthwell, Bewcastle and the Northumbrian crosses

It is, despite all my strictures, proper to start any study of Anglo-Saxon free-standing sculpture with the most famous piece of all, the Ruthwell Cross, which was found in pieces in the parish churchyard of that name in Dumfries. It was thrown down at the time of the Reformation, but (apart from the upper portion of the head) is now happily restored inside the church. Arguments about the correctness of its restoration need not detain us. The cross stands about 5 m high and the two main faces are ornamented with panels and with texts descriptive of at least some of the scenes portrayed in the panels. The cross also bears a contemporary inscription in runic characters which relates the core of 'The Dream of the Rood', one of the most moving poems in the English language. The main scene on the cross shows Christ as Judge, trampling upon the lion and adder. On the opposite side is a panel of similar size showing Christ as a symbol of Forgiveness – complementary to the role of Judge. Other scenes include the Healing of the Blind Man, Martha and Mary, Paul and Anthony in the Desert, the Annunciation, the Flight into Egypt, the Crucifixion, possibly the Nativity, St John the Baptist (although it has been recently suggested that this is God the Father) and various smaller scenes and Evangelist symbols. It is a highly sophisticated schema, highly literate in its texts and complicated in its iconography – almost an academician's monument. A new study of the cross is now being undertaken, but in broad outline these identifications are accepted.

Closely related to this monument is the cross at Bewcastle, Cumberland, which has probably stood in the same spot since it was erected (although the head has been missing since the seventeenth century). Bewcastle has a similar – but not identical – iconographical schema to that found on the Ruthwell monument, the major difference being that St John is given greater prominence, the panels are grander and the figures more elongated. Further, figural scenes occur only on the front face of the cross. A runic inscription, now much weathered, has in the past been used to associate the cross with a sub-king, Alchfrid, but this has been rejected with good reason by Raymond Page on the basis of a detailed epigraphical study. Once a fixed point in the art-historical sequence of Anglo-Saxon Christian art, this cross has now lost its firm date. On linguistic grounds Page has been tempted to date this cross, with Ruthwell, to 750–850, but even such a dating is tentative, although Farrell has emphasized 'the overwhelming modern consensus for a date *circa* 800'.

69

70

72–4

72

72–4 The Bewcastle Cross:
front, back and detail of one side.
Height of cross: c.4.4 m. (St Cuthbert,
Bewcastle, Cumberland)

Both Ruthwell and Bewcastle bear panels of running plant-scroll. On the two sides of the former are inhabited scrolls, whereas on Bewcastle there is much more variety. An inhabited plant-scroll covers the whole of one side while formal plant-scrolls appear in panels on both the other side and the back of the cross. Other patterns include a chequer design and a series of panels of interlace ornament. Further, one of the plant-scroll panels includes a sun-dial. If anything, ornament on the Ruthwell Cross is handled more competently than that on the Bewcastle Cross, but such a judgement is subjective. The slightly elongated figure style at Bewcastle is perhaps paralleled by the exaggerated and clumsy figure of the woman washing Christ's feet on the Ruthwell Cross. What is clear is that these two crosses belong to the same school of Northumbrian ornament and, if we agree with Page's linguistic arguments, it might be possible to place them in the late eighth century, a date which would chime with the rather degenerate beasts in the plant-scroll on the east face of the Ruthwell Cross. Saxl, however, attempted to identify two hands at work on the Ruthwell Cross – an unlikely thesis but one which might complicate any attempt to place the two monuments in series.

Little of the ornament of the Ruthwell Cross can be related to manuscript art. This needs emphasizing, for too often it is (because of its geographical position and undoubted quality) placed in close relation to the Lindisfarne Gospels. The interlace on the Bewcastle Cross can be paralleled without too much difficulty in Northumbrian manuscripts, but it is not distinctive enough to be given a firm date. Similarly, although many scholars start their discussion of sculpture with these two crosses, there is no evidence – rather the contrary – that these were early in the Northumbrian series and no evidence that they were the *fons et origo* of Anglo-Saxon sculptural art. Because of their completeness, their great fame through many centuries, their geographical isolation, and because of their elaborate iconography, it is easy to be lured into thinking that they are the model of early Anglo-Saxon sculpture.

In fact there is much material of similar – even better – quality. One piece which is merely a fragment and which is perhaps not so sensitive in its figural style is the stone from Aberlady, East Lothian. Here it might be possible to compare ornamental elements with insular manuscripts. One face, for example, bears interlaced birds not unlike those in the Lindisfarne Gospels, as well as a fret pattern. These patterns continue as late as the mid- to late eighth century in manuscripts, but this is perhaps as near as we get to a clear relationship to manuscript ornament of the first half of the century. (It is interesting and important, for example, that the sculpture found at Lindisfarne itself has little, if any, relationship to the manuscripts ascribed to the same monastery.) The plant-scroll on the Aberlady Cross is rather stiff, shows bunches of grapes and harks back to Near Eastern or classical forms.

Further south, at Hexham, is the monument known as Acca's Cross, said to have been set up after Bishop Acca's death in 740. It has already been pointed out that there is no evidence for such a firm dating, but the cross itself must be of eighth-century date with its carefully designed – if rather weakly-executed – vine-scrolls. Here there is no figural sculpture, no animal or interlace ornament, a rejection of all that was traditional in Hiberno-Saxon art. It depends completely on Mediterranean art and one is tempted to see this as an early – perhaps one of the earliest – attempts to represent both the Cross and Christ in almost iconoclastic vein on one monument. Other crosses reflect this

75 The Aberlady Cross fragment. Height 60 cm. (Carlowrie Castle, Lothian)

76 Acca's Cross.
Height 3.57 m. (Hexham Abbey,
Northumberland)

77 Lowther Cross.
From Lowther, Westmorland. Height
1.52 m. (London, British Museum)

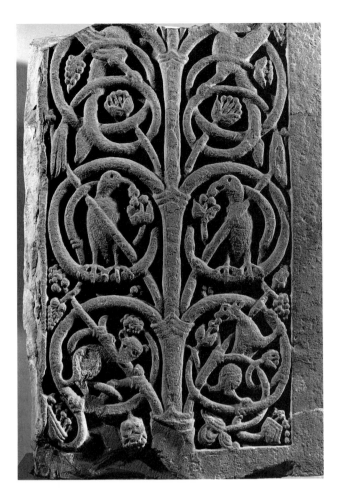

77   same purity of idea, notably the cross from Lowther, Westmorland (now in the British Museum). It is my opinion that Acca's Cross represents an early phase of the development of the plant-scroll in England. How early cannot be said, perhaps even earlier than the death of Acca. What is also clear is that the plain plant-scroll continued well on into the ninth century (a cross from Lancaster, for example) and traces survive into the tenth century.

    Such early dating cannot, as has been said, be substantiated and Romano-British inhabited vine-scrolls found in the north of England could well have provided a model for Ruthwell, Bewcastle and other inhabited scrolls. In discussing inhabited plant-scrolls we are in any case demonstrating regional differences; Ruthwell's similarity to Bewcastle has already been noted. In Yorkshire we get some common taste between the crosses at Otley and others 82 which have similar Late Antique mannerisms, as at Ilkley (only a dozen or so 83 miles away) and Easby. Is it possible that a general chronology is being 80, 81 confused with regional differentiation?

    It is also fair to mention the inhabited tree-scrolls from Jedburgh, 78 Roxburghshire, and Croft, Yorkshire. The first is classically disposed with 79 naturalistic birds and animals and well constructed wyverns in a well rounded, plastic form reminiscent of the vine-scroll at Ruthwell. The other is flatter, more sketchily and imprecisely drawn, the whole looking more like a rough version of the Gandersheim Casket. Does a century separate these two pieces, 58, 59 is it the ability of craftsmen or even geography which divides them?

80, 81 Details of the Easby Cross.
From Easby, Yorkshire. (London, Victoria and Albert
Museum)

78

82 Fragment of a cross-shaft in the
church of All Saints, Otley, Yorkshire

83 Three cross-shafts in All Saints,
Ilkley, Yorkshire. Height of tallest
shaft 3 m

84, 85 Details from the friezes built into the later church at Breedon-on-the-Hill, Leicestershire: inhabited plant-scrolls, degenerate spirals and plant-scrolls. Height 23 cm (*above*) and 18 cm (*below*)

84–7

The sculpture of the Midlands

Mercian sculpture again shows different characteristics. The most important (and probably the earliest) group comprises the friezes from Breedon-on-the-Hill, Leicestershire. The main body of carvings, now reset in a later church, consists of a large range of fragments of friezes of a type which must ultimately derive from the similar strip-work seen on the churches of the Near East. The ornament of the friezes takes various forms, the most dominant motifs being plant-scrolls; some of them inhabited, some more simple. In some the birds and animals dominate the pattern so that the scroll has almost disappeared. In these panels, and others which portray men, there is a freedom of movement and expression rarely encountered in Anglo-Saxon sculpture. Fret patterns and scalloped ornament complete the canon. Rosemary Cramp has pointed to the primacy of the Breedon sculptures in Mercia and has dated them to the reign of Offa (757–96), or at least to the late eighth century.

Breedon (founded in 675) was an important place; earlier in the eighth century it had almost certainly produced an archbishop of Canterbury, Tatwine of Briudun, and its importance is perhaps emphasized by the quality of its art, for Breedon provides us with by far the greatest surviving corpus of Anglo-Saxon architectural sculpture from a single site. Whether it is all of one period is however open to question and the fascination with Offa can be overdone: political acumen and power do not necessarily lead to innovatory art or learning (as witness the fact that Alcuin was the product of Northumbria in decline). At least one panel is closely paralleled by nearby sculpture at Fletton and could be tenth century, but the Breedon frieze must as a whole be of eighth-century date, although the sculptures might have been carved at any time during that century. Let us not be mesmerized by Offa.

Among the motifs found in the sculpture at Breedon are fret and interlace patterns which are similar in many respects to those which occur in the early Northumbrian manuscripts. A particular parallel is provided by the ribbon ornament which is regularly placed and runs continuously from one nodus to the next (one wonders if it could originally have been painted in different colours to tease the eye as was the case in the Northumbrian manuscripts). The fret ornament occurs on the same piece of stone as an inhabited plant-scroll of rather tendril-like character, which is seen more clearly elsewhere. The same scroll (although here inhabited by riders) is contiguous with a degenerate trumpet-spiral pattern. It is not without interest that spiral patterns were dying out in manuscript art by the last half of the eighth century and rarely occur in sculpture, particularly in Northumbria (although they are known on Pictish, Scottish and Irish monuments). In England they occur most frequently in Mercia (on the font at Deerhurst, Gloucestershire, for example), and at South Kyme, Lincolnshire. South Kyme has produced a number of fragments of high quality and great importance. Unfortunately it is impossible to say whether they all come from the same object because they are cemented firmly into the wall of the present church. Here are spirals, a regular fret pattern, a plant scroll, interlace and, most interestingly, a fragment which shows an interlaced animal (also seen at Iken, Suffolk) the foot of which is closely paralleled in the Lindisfarne Gospel group.

89

86, 87 Details from the friezes at Breedon-on-the-Hill, Leicestershire: birds, animals, frets and interlace. Height of both details 23 cm

88 Panel from Breedon-on-the-Hill, Leicestershire. Possibly the Virgin. Height 53 cm

89 Detail from the friezes at Breedon-on-the-Hill, Leicestershire: inhabited plant-scroll. Height 23 cm

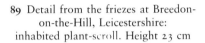

90 Panel from Breedon-on-the-Hill, Leicestershire. Probably part of a sarcophagus. Height 20 cm

91, 92 Two panels from Breedon-on-the-Hill, Leicestershire.
Left: two figures (height 49 cm); *right*: an angel (height 91 cm)

94 Part of a frieze with an angel and plant-scrolls, at St Margaret, Fletton, Huntingdonshire

93 The Hedda Stone, Peterborough Cathedral.
Length *c*.1 m

95 Grave slab at Wirksworth, Derbyshire, showing scenes from the Passion. Length: 2 m

Panels bearing figures which are assumed to be of eighth-century date are reasonably common in Mercia. The most remarkable examples are on the stone grave-cover, known as the Hedda Stone, in Peterborough Cathedral. This is so worn that it can no longer be properly illustrated. But it is clear that the roof is similar in its ornamental repertoire to that seen on the Gandersheim Casket. Within arches on the long sides of the stone are a series of twelve nimbed figures, remarkably similar to two figures seen elsewhere in the cathedral and closely paralleled at Fletton. At Breedon two figures within a panel, which are less stiff and formalized, seem to belong to the same group of carvings as the rather tendril-like inhabited plant-scroll. There is a liveliness about these Mercian figures which is not found on the crosses from Ruthwell and Bewcastle or indeed on any other Northumbrian monuments. They may not be so competent in their treatment of volume and mass, but in their own way they are equally great works of art.

It is clear that there were other hands at work among the stone carvers of Breedon – some of which are of later date. One piece – a panel showing an angel – is probably of the late ninth century. The angel breaks out of the frame in a manner similar to that of the later Winchester style (below, p. 154ff.), although it is by no means typical of that style. Elsewhere at Breedon are fragments of a sarcophagus of coarse quality which, although they have been compared to the Book of Cerne, are frankly uninformative; another wall panel displaying a half-length figure of the Virgin is also of poor quality. Other hands – perhaps slightly later – possibly produced some of the plain plant-scrolls. This latter work may, however, be no more than the product of a less competent mason; if this is indeed so it points a moral for those who would try to date sculpture on the basis of quality alone.

There is no definite evidence for the priority of either Mercian or Northumbrian stone sculpture. Monuments take different forms in different areas. The architectural sculpture at Breedon, Fletton and South Kyme is more varied than the architectural sculpture of Northumbria, whilst free-standing crosses seem to be more common in Northumbria. Quality is about as even and as varied in both areas and dating on stylistic grounds is equally impossible. Parallels are drawn with manuscript illumination, but the examples adduced are almost useless. The only significant chronological feature is that the trumpet-spiral apparently dies out towards the end of the eighth century in England (but not in Ireland). However, lack of firm evidence does not deter the optimistic from dating sculpture.

There is, then, a considerable range of motif and pattern in the sculpture. One strange piece deserves especial mention. A slab, perhaps from a funerary monument, from Wirksworth, Derbyshire, has an extremely primitive figural style. It also has a splendid iconography which demonstrates some of the sources of Anglo-Saxon theology. Two scenes appear to be missing on the left-hand side; the other scenes include Mary washing the feet of Christ, the Crucifixion, the Death of the Virgin, the Presentation, the Descent into Hell, the Ascension, the Annunciation and possibly a representation of Pentecost. A strange mix, with Byzantine and Mediterranean overtones. Chronologically little can be said about the stone: it fits well into the Mercian milieu of the pre-Viking period and the nature of its iconography perhaps gives us a taste of one of the most eclectic monuments of this period, the Franks Casket.

The Franks Casket – secular iconography?

The Franks Casket is a rectangular bone box (23 × 13 × 19 cm), discovered in a private house in Auzon, Haute Loire, France, in the nineteenth century. All but the right-hand end (which is now in the Bargello in Florence) were presented by Sir Augustus Wollaston Franks to the British Museum in 1867. (The donor was the Museum's greatest benefactor, and attempts to call it the Auzon Casket should be resisted by all right-thinking scholars!) The sides are inscribed with an Old English text in runic characters and (in one place) with a

95

34–7

96 Side panel from the Franks Casket, now separated from the rest (see pls. 34–7). The subject has not been interpreted. (Florence, Museo del Bargello)

97 Fragment of a bone plaque from Larling, Norfolk, showing Romulus and Remus. Length 7 cm. (Norwich, Castle Museum)

Latin text in mixed runic and insular scripts. Scenes portrayed are not all identifiable but include subjects as diverse as Romulus and Remus, Weland the Smith, the Adoration of the Magi, the sack of Jerusalem by Titus, a lost Old English legend concerning Egil, and other scenes which might have a Germanic origin. The source for this strange iconography is generally agreed to be some sort of illustrated universal history (the Alexandrian *Scaliger Barbarus* written at Corbie – a monastery much influenced by the Anglo-Saxons – is mentioned in this context) with Germanic additions perhaps taken from painted or carved wooden panels. Leslie Webster has, however, also pointed out that its form is almost certainly derived from that of Late Antique boxes and suggests such an object, perhaps made in a Germanic workshop, as its model.

Elisabeth Okasha dates the casket to the eighth century on epigraphic grounds, and Leslie Webster's analysis of the ornament confirms a close harmony – in its rather coarse technique – with Northumbrian art of the first half of the eighth century or perhaps, on the basis of the foliate motifs, the middle of that century. However coarse the execution of the ornament, the intellectual range of this object is formidable. It could well reflect the academic and historical interests of the Northumbrian schoolmen at York or in one of the major monasteries of the Bedan or post-Bedan period. It may not be a product of a religious centre, but great learning would be needed to construct its iconography. It is not without interest that another bone plaque (a fragment of a larger object), from Larling, Norfolk, bears a Romulus and Remus scene, together with animal ornament of a slightly more degenerate character than that which occurs on the Gandersheim Casket.

97

The end of the Northumbrian manuscript tradition

In a period of great intellectual activity in England; in a century which saw the death of Bede and the birth of Alcuin, and which also produced high quality poetry and imaginative prose, it is strange that it is only in sculpture that innovatory ideas appear: figural sculpture of sophisticated exegetical character, as at Ruthwell, or of universal history, as displayed on the Franks Casket. Manuscript art as it survives is rich but arid of ideas. It is typical, for example, that the influence of the Lindisfarne Gospels is still clearly evident in the second half of the eighth century. And strongly evident. But, as has been pointed out, most of the surviving illuminated books from the first three centuries of English Christianity are grand service books, Bibles, psalters and so on. Few of them are books of the study and only one of those so far discussed – the Leningrad Bede – has been an historical work. That other books existed is of course clear, some perhaps (like the cosmographical codex which we know to have been given by Ceolfrid to King Aldfrith of Northumbria) of Mediterranean origin. There were presumably illustrated histories and scientific works, but none survive and it is not until the tenth century that more varied illustrated literature occurs. Metalwork is scrappy at this period, but here and there (as on the Fuller Brooch, p. 110) we gain an impression of a wider interest, a wider intellectual curiosity. We are missing through accident or usage a whole area of illustrative art which almost certainly existed. If Corbie – closely in touch with insular centres – was producing such wide-ranging chronicles as the *Scaliger Barbarus* there seems no reason to suppose that Northumbrian *scriptoria* were not able to cope with similar material. If manuscripts had survived from eighth-century York they might have provided us with such material. Indeed, if the Durham Cassiodorus was produced in York, it might be that we can gain an inkling of how a major Anglo-Saxon book of the study might have appeared.

While not so inventive, manuscript art still provides colourful and complicated patterns. Consider, for example, the Lichfield Gospels (sometimes known as the St Chad Gospels). Not so big as Lindisfarne, it is still an impressive book, measuring *c*.31 × 23.5 cm. It is incomplete; much of St Luke's Gospel and the whole of St John's are missing. No canon tables or prefaces survive, but we have one carpet page, two Evangelist portraits, a page with the four Evangelists' symbols, four large initials and a number of framed pages. The book has probably been in Lichfield Cathedral since the tenth century, but it spent part of its early career in Wales, being given in the ninth century to the church of Llandeilo Fawr, Carmarthenshire (in exchange for a horse). The ornament is of high quality; the colours have been abraded, but include yellow, light blue, brown and green, with violet/mauve as the main colour. But although high artistry is achieved, the drawings of human figures are particularly inept – or should one say non-representational? The pages with initials are rather more splendid and they, and the display scripts which go with them, have a runic-like angularity of character. Undoubtedly the most splendid ornament occurs on the surviving carpet page, which is clearly related in form and ornament to those of the Lindisfarne Gospels. The bird and animal ornament is perhaps less happily placed on the page and the angularity of the interlaced bird designs is distinctly at odds with the flowing patterns of the Lindisfarne Gospels (perhaps even foreshadowing the angular interlacing of the Book of Kells). Wendy Stein, in an unpublished thesis, has made an extensive study of the manuscript and with great caution has suggested a date *c*.730. Her argument being that 'the ornament of Lindisfarne pulls Lichfield back in date towards the beginning of the eighth century. Their *incipit*, carpet pages and zoomorphic ornament are too similar to be separated by as much as two generations.' She favours a provincial Northumbrian or Mercian origin for the book.

There has been too much looking back in attempts to date the Lichfield Gospels. There is obviously no prototype in Ireland for this manuscript, but eyes have been cast longingly in the direction of Iona, the most likely place for the production of the Book of Kells (below, p. 129). The Kells parallels to Lichfield are as close as those of Lindisfarne and, as the generally accepted date

98 Initial (XPI) from the Lichfield Gospels, p. 5 (Lichfield, Cathedral Library)

99 *Opposite*: the opening of St Luke's Gospel. The Lichfield Gospels, p. 221 (Lichfield, Cathedral Library). *c*.31 × 23.5 cm

155

for the Book of Kells is late eighth century, there seems no good reason to date Lichfield as early as 730. The angularity of the display script and the initials, the angularity of the interlaced bird patterns and the portrayal of the human face all seem to fit more easily with Kells. Only the XPI initial on p. 5 of the manuscript points directly at Lindisfarne – but then so it does in Kells. While preferring a later date, I would not be disturbed by the more commonly accepted 'second quarter of the eighth century'. As a pendant to the argument as to provenance, I would see the runic-like display script as a conscious imitation of the runic alphabet; if so, it is more likely to have been carried out in Northumbria (where runes abound) than in Mercia, where runes are known only in peripheral areas. Is there indeed in the Lichfield Gospels some conscious antiquarianism on the part of a scribe looking back to a golden age?

Other books have been given a provenance and date similar to the Lichfield Gospels. It is almost certain that two of them, represented by the Maaseik Gospel fragments, were painted on the Continent – both these books seem palaeographically to belong to a continental centre (perhaps Echternach) under strong Anglo-Saxon influence. One important Gospel Book does, however, remain firmly anchored in a Northumbrian or northern Mercian centre – the Leningrad Gospels (Leningrad, Public Library, Cod.F.v.I.8). Most palaeographers agree that it belongs to the second half of the eighth century (although in some cases such a dating depends on a mid-eighth-century date for the Book of Kells, a date which is accepted by very few scholars). Julian Brown and E. A. Lowe have both agreed that it is Northumbrian, an opinion

98

HIC IohaNNES f hu NI TE

IN MA TA

HIC IO NIS FRO A QVI VE U TEM LAIH HAN FIT IN

which is supported in general terms by the ornament. (A scratched runic inscription would suggest that it was in Northumbria at an early period.) The manuscript measures 35 × 24 cm and is ornamented on twelve pages of canon tables (which show construction marks) and on four pages of major initials. Smaller initials for prefaces and chapters also occur. The colours, which are rich and varied, include green, orange, yellow and mauve. Most striking however are blues and browns. The brown is particularly marked in the page illustrated, where the great animal in the loop of the letter is not unlike in its stance and interlace the animals of the Witham Pins or even the Gandersheim Casket. The interlace in the panels of the frame and the animals in the corner panels all hark back to Lindisfarne, but are looser and less disciplined. The display script is loose and freer in style than anything we have seen earlier, some serifs terminating in very fine hair spirals, others in animal heads – in the interior of some of the smaller initials are animal heads not unlike some in Mercian or southern English metalwork. There is also a southern element in the display script and in the infill of the letter R of the word LIBER. To make a bold guess one might place this manuscript in southern Northumbria – in York perhaps (to which every scholar of the period would wish to consign so much) or in one of the rich monasteries like Whitby, which certainly produced metalwork of a similar ornamental character.

Southern illumination

It is about the middle of the eighth century that the first major southern English ornamented manuscripts to survive appear. The Vespasian Psalter (British Library, Cotton Vespasian A.I) and the Stockholm *Codex Aureus* (Royal Library, A.135) are both assigned to Kent. The Vespasian Psalter has been the subject of extensive recent study by David Wright, whose vast knowledge of contemporary manuscripts is perhaps unequalled. Wright, however, notoriously dates things early and his dating of the Vespasian Psalter is no exception. The surviving illuminations in this manuscript include a full-page representation of David, with musicians and scribes enthroned beneath an arch, and a number of elaborate initials, including two historiated examples (David and Jonathan and David killing the lion). The varied colours include gold and silver. Wright considers that it is modelled on a sixth-century Italian manuscript of Byzantine influence, one entirely different from the Northumbrian series. It was almost certainly written and painted by one hand at St Augustine's Abbey, Canterbury. Wright dates it to the 720s, others, more convincingly, to *c*.775. Wright's judgement illustrates the chronological problems of the manuscript art of the eighth century – there are no fixed points. Let us, then, examine the group of rich manuscripts of south English origin which include the Stockholm *Codex Aureus*, the Book of Cerne (Cambridge, University Library, Ll.I.10), a Bede manuscript (British Library, Cotton Tiberius C.ii), the Barberini Gospels (Vatican, Biblioteca Apostolica, Barb.lat.570) and the Canterbury Bible (British Library, Royal 1. E. VI) – sometimes known as the Canterbury Gospels. They are usually said to have been produced in that order, but the dates to which scholars attribute them vary. It is likely that they all come from Kent (or at least from south-east England). (A Mercian origin has been suggested from time to time for the Book of Cerne, but Kuhn's wholesale attribution of much of this group to Mercia has not been taken seriously.)

100 *Opposite*: portrait and symbol of St John from the Book of Cerne (Cambridge, University Library, Ll.I.10, fol. 31v). 23 × 18 cm

110

112

101, 102 *Pages 92, 93*: canon table and (*right*) portrait and symbol of St Matthew, from the Stockholm *Codex Aureus* (Stockholm, Royal Library, A.135, ff. 8v, 9v). 40 × 31 cm

100

Two of these – the *Codex Aureus* and the Canterbury Bible – are very grand manuscripts indeed, having purple pages and rich illumination. The Stockholm *Codex Aureus* is a Kentish manuscript; an ingenious, but complicated, hypothesis argues convincingly that it was painted not at Canterbury (to which it was given after being ransomed from the Danes in the ninth century) but at some other Kentish centre. It measures 40 × 31 cm, has eight pages of canon tables, two surviving Evangelist portraits, four completely decorated initial pages and various other elaborate initials. The text of the Gospels is written on alternate white and purple-stained pages (white, gold, silver and red being used for the text on these pages). Most remarkable is the great XPI monogram page, where the gold letters in classical capitals appear almost as single metal letters set in a frame, in some cases even as though supported behind by a bar. The Evangelist portraits may have been modelled on those of the St Augustine Gospels (see above, p. 29). Like the Vespasian Psalter, this manuscript displays (for the last time in insular art) developed trumpet spiral patterns. Interlace and animal designs, together with meander patterns and foliate capitals, complete the ornamental repertoire. Here is seen the final movement of the animal ornament away from the Lindisfarne tradition of neatly looped animals with elongated necks and bodies, to the tradition of small, compact, dog-like creatures which were to predominate in the ninth century. The two traditions occur here but there is perhaps a feeling that the latter is more favoured.

These same animals are seen in the Canterbury Bible, a fragmentary book which measures 47 × 34.5 cm (nearly as big as the Codex Amiatinus), almost certainly written and painted at St Augustine's Abbey, Canterbury, and one of the grandest surviving English Bibles – although only a portion of the Gospels now remains. The surviving illumination consists of five pages of canon tables and the initial page of St Mark's Gospel – the Evangelist portraits are missing. A very grand series of pages with formal, impeccably classical, display scripts. Gold, silver, orange, green and black are the dominating colours; there are also purple pages. It resembles the more splendid Gospel Books of the Carolingian Court school and must have been influenced by them, as by a Late Antique Bible (the lost *Bible of St Gregory*), which is known to have been at St Augustine's at this time.

The animal ornament in the canon tables in the Canterbury Bible and the similar ornament in the initial B of Cotton Tiberius C.ii give some chronological clues. The animals are delineated in black and white, often have speckled bodies and fit by contortion into small fields. Some of the bodies degenerate into plant scrolls with rounded leaves (seen particularly in Cotton Tiberius C.ii). Similar animals are found on ninth-century metalwork, particularly on objects found in the hoards from Trewhiddle, Cornwall, and Beeston Tor, Derbyshire. These objects are made of silver and the animal and vegetal ornament is executed in shallow carving against a black niello background and is constrained within small panels (at Trewhiddle in triangular fields). They either imitate the manuscript designs or *vice versa*. In view of the colours – black and white – used in the manuscripts it seems likely (as was the case in the Book of Durrow) that the manuscripts followed the metalwork. This is not to say that the manuscripts discussed here post-date Trewhiddle or Beeston Tor, rather that the style recognized in these two hoards was the origin of the style found in the manuscripts.

94

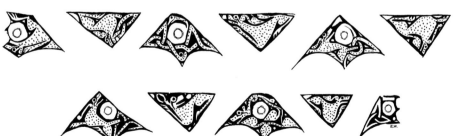

103 Enlarged detail from a canon table
of the Canterbury Bible
(London, British Library, Royal 1.E.VI,
fol. 4r)

104 Animal ornament from horn
mounts, Trewhiddle, St Austell,
Cornwall (see pl. 119)

105, 106 Ornament of finger rings of
Æthelwulf and Æthelswith (see pls.
117, 118)

Trewhiddle and its contemporaries

Trewhiddle was buried with coins dated *c.*872–5, Beeston Tor with coins dated *c.*875. This means that the two hoards were laid down at this date, but there is no way of telling when the objects themselves were made. It is, however, not without interest that at least two other hoards contain objects decorated in this style – Talnotrie, Kirkcudbrightshire (*c.*875), and Cuerdale, Lancashire (*c.*903). These dates demonstrate that the style was still about in the late ninth century. A hoard from Hon, Norway, which includes a gold finger-ring ornamented in the same style, might indicate a rather earlier date as the gold coins in it were collected together *c.*855–60, but the date of deposition is difficult to estimate. Finger-rings bearing the names of two historical personages, King Æthelwulf (839–58) and Queen Æthelswith (853/4–888/9), which bear motifs executed in this style confirm its mid- to late ninth-century date. A new find from Pentney, Norfolk, consisting of six disc brooches, shortly to be published by Leslie Webster, does, however, show a vast range of difference within the style. Some motifs are perhaps more closely related to the Witham Pins, others are close to the Trewhiddle mounts.

The Trewhiddle style was still firmly in use in the second half of the ninth century and yet in its earliest form must date much earlier. Similarly there is a consensus that the Canterbury Bible and the Book of Cerne and Cotton Tiberius C.ii all belong before 850. But firm evidence for this dating is non-existent. It is clear that the Stockholm *Codex Aureus* and the Vespasian Psalter are earlier; but how much earlier cannot be said. They are, however, so closely related in their ornament that they must be considered together even if they are (as Wright would have it) a generation apart. There is a tendency by students of the manuscripts of this period to space the material evenly out over the period between the Lindisfarne Gospels and the Canterbury Bible, setting them down as groups or single books every twenty-five years or so. Such scholars will not admit of bunching; they see a steady development, a continuous and even growth. But it could as easily be argued that the manuscripts do not develop in this even manner. There is no reason, on the present evidence, why all the manuscripts from the Vespasian Psalter onwards should not be bunched together in two groups, one say from 750–75 and the other from 825–50. There would be no evidence for such dating either, but palaeographers are strangely reluctant to leave a single generation without a grand manuscript in the eighth century, although they seem quite happy to leave three-quarters of a century between the Canterbury Gospels and the next great manuscript, the Corpus Christi version of Bede's *Life of St Cuthbert*. There is some justification in historical terms for such a position: King Alfred himself lamented the falling off of learning in England during his reign. This is a strong contemporary argument. But then even kings can exaggerate and, in any case, Alfred encouraged learning by his own example and it would be strange indeed if grand books were not produced for this great king and his great successors, Edward and Athelstan. There was wealth in England at this time, despite the Viking invasions, and art is not necessarily adversely affected by troubled times if patrons and will survive. What is badly needed is to attack the problem of the chronology of the eighth- and ninth-century manuscripts from all sides, from the points of view of palaeographers, historians, textual critics and style historians, in order to hammer out a chronology agreeable to all parties and not just based on the special pleading of a single discipline.

117
118
120

107–9 The embroidered *casula* of St
Harlindis and St Relindis (*above left*),
with details of the embroidery (*left and
above right*). Length of *casula* 87 cm
(St Catherine, Maaseik, Belgium). See
p. 108

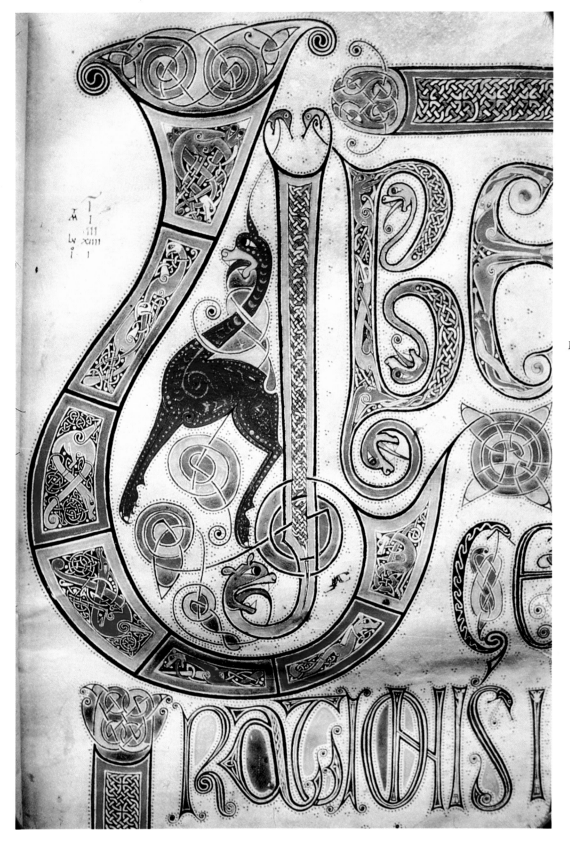

110 Initial L of St Matthew's Gospel, from the Leningrad Gospels (Leningrad, Public Library, Cod. F.v.I.8, fol. 18r). See p. 88

III Initial B from a
manuscript of Bede's
Ecclesiastical history
(London, British Library,
Cotton Tiberius C.ii, fol.
5v). See p. 94

112 Portrait of King David, from the Vespasian Psalter (London, British Library, Cotton Vespasian A.I, fol. 30v). See p. 91

113 Part of St Matthew's Gospel, from the Stockholm *Codex Aureus* (Stockholm, Royal Library, A.135, fol. 11r). See p. 94

114 *Opposite*: canon table from the Canterbury Bible (London, British Library, Royal 1.E.VI, fol. 43r). 47 × 34.5 cm. See p. 94

116 Openwork brooch from Beeston Tor, Derbyshire.
Diameter 4.9 cm (London, British Museum). See p. 94

115 The Strickland Brooch.
Diameter 11 cm (London, British Museum). See p. 100

117, 118 Two royal rings.
Left: King Æthelwulf's ring, inscribed with his name,
from near Laverstock, Wiltshire. Diameter 2.8 cm.
Right: Queen Æthelswith's ring, decorated with the
agnus dei, from Aberford, Yorkshire (London, British
Museum). See p. 96

119 Two curved horn-mounts, from Trewhiddle,
Cornwall.
Length of largest mount 21.4 cm (London, British
Museum). See p. 94

120 *Right*: six disc brooches discovered at Pentney,
Norfolk.
Diameter of largest brooch 10.2 cm (London, British
Museum). See p. 96

121, 122 Two views of the Alfred Jewel.
The inscription reads AELFRED MEC HEHT GEWYRCAN
(Alfred ordered me to be made). For the back, see pl.
191. Length 7.5 cm (Oxford, Ashmolean Museum).
See p. 110

123 Gold plaque from Brandon, Suffolk, showing St
John the Evangelist as an eagle-headed figure.
Height 3.4 cm (London, British Museum). See p. 111

The Wolverhampton Pillar – a chronological enigma

The intractable nature of the chronology of the sculpture has already been referred to, but a sculptural tradition did ride behind the manuscript and metalwork art. The material is diverse, often of poor quality, worn or *sui generis*. One of the grandest monuments is, however, so worn that it is now virtually impossible to distinguish the details of the ornament. This is the Wolverhampton round-shaft. Here is displayed (and can still be faintly seen, particularly on the cast taken in the 1880s for the Victoria and Albert Museum) something of the same panelled style seen in the Canterbury Bible and on the Trewhiddle horn mounts and the same or related animal ornament. It also bears an acanthus-like leaf ornament which is clearly derived from Carolingian prototypes. Kendrick has called this piece 'the noblest monument that has come down to us from the pre-Alfredian sculptures of the West Saxon supremacy'. He associates it with Æthelwulf or his sons. It is unparalleled, only palely reflected in some more northerly round-shafts, like that from Masham, Yorkshire. In my view this object must be placed late in the ninth century. It has tenth-century traits (a date suggested for it most recently by Rosemary Cramp), the birds in some of the triangular fields being very similar to those that appear, for example, on the Canterbury censer-cover, which is usually considered to be of tenth-century date. A date within twenty-five years of 900 would be perfectly acceptable for the Wolverhampton Pillar.

The Wolverhampton Pillar stands in a close relationship to Trewhiddle and the Canterbury Bible and a long way from Ruthwell and Bewcastle. Nearer to them lies the cross-shaft from Easby, Yorkshire. The delicate deep-cut carving of this sculpture, with its splendid formalized vine-scroll, its representation of the Apostles and a Christ in Majesty, is in the true Northumbrian tradition. The animals in the scroll, however, are quite close to those of the Trewhiddle group and particularly to the animals in the scrolls which lead up to the Canterbury Bible. The scroll itself has parallels with Carolingian ornament.

The Easby Cross is the finest example of a group of crosses from Northumbria which includes the Rothbury fragments (now in the University Museum of Antiquities of Newcastle-upon-Tyne); the possibly slightly earlier cross No. 1 from Otley, Yorkshire; the finely drawn but much corroded crosses from Ilkley, Yorkshire; the coarser crosses from Nunnykirk, Northumberland and Lowther, Westmorland; and the even coarser examples from Eyam, Yorkshire, and Bakewell, Derbyshire. In Mercia, while nothing achieves the splendour of the Wolverhampton Pillar, there is a group of sculptures which must belong to this earlier period. Foremost are the cross-head from Cropthorne, Worcestershire, cross-shafts from Gloucester and Newent, Gloucestershire, a fragmentary slab from Acton Beauchamp, Herefordshire, and a slab from Wroxeter, Shropshire. The Cropthorne fragment displays a vine-scroll which is so degenerate that it has almost disappeared; it is dominated by birds and dog-like animals closely comparable with those found in the south English manuscripts. It was creatures like these which were to be taken over and converted into something very different through Scandinavian influence, as at St Alkmund, Derby (see below, p. 146). With the exception of the St Alkmund Cross, all these crosses could date to any period within a bracket of say 780 and 880. Typologically there is little to say. Mercia and Northumbria seem to have had different stylistic traits.

124, 125 The Wolverhampton Pillar and (*above*) an expanded drawing of part of the ornament, made in the nineteenth century.
Height *c.*3.6 m. (Churchyard of St Peter, Wolverhampton)

126 Cross-head from Cropthorne, Worcestershire.
Height 84 cm

127, 128 Two sides of a cross-shaft from Nunnykirk,
Northumberland.
Height 1.3 m. (Newcastle, University Museum of
Antiquities)

131 Cross-shaft at Masham,
Yorkshire.
Height 2 m

129, 130 *Left*: fragments of a cross-
shaft from Rothbury, Northumberland.
Height 38 cm. (Newcastle, University
Museum of Antiquities)

132, 133 Back and front of a grave-marker in All Hallows, Whitchurch, Hampshire.
Height 57 cm

Sculpture in the south

The sculpture of England south of Mercia hardly forms a coherent group. A grave-marker from Whitchurch, Hampshire, which bears a memorial inscription to a lady named Fridburga, has on the back an incised tree-scroll with terminal leaves which is related in many respects to the metalwork of *c*.800. The front bears a half-length nimbed figure (possibly of Christ). Other sculpture from Colerne, Wiltshire; Shaftesbury, Dorset; West Camel, Somerset, and so on seem to relate (as has been pointed out by Rosemary Cramp) to the Mercian group discussed above. The architectural sculpture from Britford, Wiltshire, consists largely of a highly conventionalized formal plant-scroll which, as it bears no lush acanthus ornament, must date from before say 900. The backward-looking animals in the shaft fragment at Ramsbury, Wiltshire, might be related to animals in the Canterbury Bible, but they are executed in a rather ham-fisted manner and it is difficult to date them within a century. If there is an element of despair in what is written here about the dating of sculpture, it is because, although we can roughly divide sculpture into eighth- and ninth-century groups, any attempt at accurate dating can only be on the basis of judgement of ornament diverse in quality and geographical location, executed by masters who might be old-fashioned perfectionists, experimental innovators, incompetents or journeymen. There is little opportunity for comparison with art in other media and (when parallels do occur) scale, wear and a very rickety chronology help little.

Textiles and metalwork

One surviving group of textiles adds a new dimension to our knowledge of the art of this period. It consists of a series of embroideries in the church of St Catherine at Maaseik, Belgium (to which they came from Aldeneik in 1571), which is at present being studied by Dominic Tweddle and Mildred Budny. They are known as the *casula* (i.e. chasuble) of St Harlindis and St Relindis and the *velamen* (veil) of St Harlindis. Remodelled in the Middle Ages, the *casula* now consists of a backing cloth on which are a group of textiles, many of which in style, ornament and colour are closely related to the Canterbury Bible and its related manuscripts. (Whether the original objects were a *casula* and *velamen* is doubtful.) The embroidered strips from the *casula* are decorated with arcades or roundels which contain animals, plant and interlace ornament, at the ends of which are monograms. All the embroidery is worked in gold and silk on a linen backing cloth (much of the gold is now missing) – the earliest known examples of *opus Anglicanum*. The *velamen*, the original use of which is debated, is less easy to identify in cultural or chronological terms. The ornament is less easy to analyse and explain; it consists mostly of tablet braids embellished with blue and green glass beads, pearls and gilded copper-alloy bosses. There seems no reason to doubt the traditional ninth-century date for these pieces.

Perhaps the most striking element in the art of the ninth century is, however, the quality and variety of the metalwork. Partly because of the Scandinavian incursions, more hoards were buried, hoards like Trewhiddle, Pentney and Beeston Tor, which have come to light over the last two hundred years to reveal the riches of the Anglo-Saxon silversmith's art. Silver had by this time become the chief medium of the jeweller; supplies of gold had gradually

132, 13

134

135

107–9

134 Fragment of architectural
sculpture in St Peter, Britford,
Wiltshire.
Height of ornamented stones 1.24 m

135 Fragments of two cross-shafts in
Holy Cross, Ramsbury, Wiltshire.
The two portions are from separate
monuments. The upper is of ninth-
century date; the lower, tenth century

become scarce during the preceding centuries and, although there had been an attempt to imitate gold by the fairly consistent use of gilding on a silver or copper alloy base during the eighth century (as on the Witham Pins), the craftsman seems to have recognized that silver (while not so valuable as gold) had qualities of its own. It was readily available in the form of the contemporary coinage (it may even have been mined in the British Isles) and it could be decorated by inlay or carving. Although the remains of the jeweller's art are few and far between, enough survives to demonstrate the high quality of the craftsmanship.

33

At the conclusion of this chapter I would like to introduce four items which demonstrate this quality and also, in one case, a remarkable secular iconography. The first piece is known as the Strickland Brooch, taking its name from its earliest recorded owner, a nineteenth-century Yorkshire antiquary. It consists of an openwork dished silver disc, some 11 cm in diameter, the surface of which is inlaid with blue glass, gold and niello. The basic design is formed of a hollow-sided cruciform figure with animal mask terminals which engage with a quatrefoil which produces further animal masks within the arms of the cross. These fields are defined by beaded borders which enclose pairs of backward looking dog-like animals divided from each other by a beaded border which, although interrupted, forms a circle concentric with the border. The face is dominated by five large collared bosses. The brooch is remarkable in that it expresses the continuing Anglo-Saxon interest in polychromy and in the interplay of light on broken surfaces. The openwork, the speckling of the gold plates, the blue glass eyes in the animal masks and the black of the niello all contrast with the basic silver surface of the brooch. These techniques are seen elsewhere in metalwork but never more effectively than on this piece.

115

1

Another disc brooch of similar form is the Fuller Brooch, named after the collector Capt. A. W. F. Fuller. Perhaps the most perfect piece of surviving Anglo-Saxon metalwork of the Christian period, it is splendid in its constraint, being of silver inlaid with niello. Five figures in the centre represent the senses – sight, hearing, smell, touch and taste – and these are surrounded by roundels containing human busts, animals and foliate motifs. The Five Senses were at least known in the Anglo-Saxon literature (Ælfric, for instance, mentions them), but they are never represented elsewhere in a context as early as this. The technical mastery of the craftsman who made the Fuller Brooch is of the highest standard for any period of the jeweller's art. Here can be seen the great competence of Late Anglo-Saxon metalworking which is too often represented by scrappy remains, detritus left after the more valuable material had been melted down.

121-2

One of the most famous pieces of Anglo-Saxon metalwork is the Alfred Jewel, a gold, enamel and crystal object which was found at Newton Park, Somerset. An inscription in the openwork gold frame reads AELFRED MEC HEHT GEWYRCAN (Alfred ordered me to be made). The terminal is in the form of a three-dimensional animal head, the mouth of which forms a socket, perhaps for a wand. (It has been identified with an otherwise unknown word æstal – presumably a pointer used by a reader – mentioned in Alfred's Old English translation of Gregory's Pastoral care.) The figure below the crystal closely resembles the figure of Sight in the Fuller Brooch, but it is most commonly thought to represent Christ as Wisdom or Christ in Majesty. The

136 Saddlebow from Coppergate, York. Length 31 cm. (York, Yorkshire Museum)

back plate is decorated with an acanthus-like plant motif. The object is usually (because of the inscription) associated with King Alfred, but it is not without interest that in a period when royal titles meant something, there is no royal title in the inscription.

Fourth, a find made by a fisherman at Brandon, Suffolk, in 1978. It is a small gold plaque embellished with niello. On the front of the object is a half-length representation of the eagle symbol of St John the Evangelist framed by an inscription which identifies the figure. Presumably from a book cover or a small standing cross (compare the symbol on the later Brussels Cross) it recalls manuscript illumination in a manner not normally found in metalwork, only perhaps matched in its fluency by the Fuller Brooch. Stylistically and epigraphically it can best be placed in southern England and related to the Canterbury group of manuscripts of the late eighth or early ninth century, but it echoes a tradition first apparent in the Lindisfarne Gospels which continues into the tenth century (consider the lettered panels on the stole of St Cuthbert).

In conclusion, a recent find from York demonstrates that much art must be missing from our corpus. The saddle bow from the Coppergate excavations is of wood inlaid with thin silver-impressed plaques which very much resemble the form and delimitation of the fields of the Trewhiddle horn mounts. The ornament in itself is not very exciting, but the material reminds us that a considerable body of art executed in wood existed and is now missing. Our evidence as always in the Anglo-Saxon period is far from complete.

123

240

1

207

136

III

4 Influences

As we move out of the ninth century, the influences which affect English art and the influences which that art had on its neighbours become clearer. Basically, English art of the tenth and eleventh centuries drew on the Carolingian and Ottonian traditions of the Continent together with an undertow carried from Byzantium and, in the north of England, from Scandinavia. During the eleventh century a certain amount of return traffic took place, particularly towards the west of France and perhaps a little towards Scandinavia. But the centuries after the Conversion tell a much more complicated story in which England was both receiver and donor. In the period when the cultural life of England (itself very vital) received influences from Rome, from Gaul, from the north and west of Britain and later from Germany, when missionaries were received and dispatched, it is hardly surprising that we are presented with a prodigious eclecticism in the art. At all times the influence appears to have been two-way and the story to be told is complicated but fascinating.

Some of this story has been recounted in the preceding chapters and some repetition will be inevitable, but the story is so remarkable that it bears re-telling in a different context. The pattern is often dimly seen and is consequently controversial. The nuances cannot be completely revealed in a book of this size. I shall, therefore, try to recount the main outlines of the story, without the use of too many conditional phrases and qualifications.

We have seen how the Church introduced into England new motifs and new media from the Continent (from Gaul and Italy in particular) and we have also seen how the influences of the earlier art of the Anglo-Saxons can be traced in the new media. We have also glimpsed the presence of Celtic motifs, particularly developed spiral ornament, and have touched on the difficulty of locating the *scriptoria* in which such manuscripts as the Book of Durrow were produced.

The developed spiral ornament

The developed spiral motif (so important in English art of the seventh and eighth centuries) had its origins in the pre-Roman Iron Age of Britain, which produced a magnificently controlled non-representational art, the tradition of which never completely died out, although it was suppressed and appears only in a muted form on a number of objects, bowls, brooches and dress fasteners in the period after the Romans had left Britain. The objects which survive are generally mean and of small scale, the style being a re-interpretation of old motifs in new circumstances. The most important body of material of the fifth to seventh centuries on which the developed spiral motif occurs comprises mounts on the hanging bowls of which the most elaborate examples were found in the Sutton Hoo ship-burial. Although most hanging-bowls are found

137 *Opposite*: standing cross at Kildalton, Islay, Argyllshire

in pre-Christian Anglo-Saxon contexts there is some evidence that they were also made in Scotland (a mould used in the manufacture of such an escutcheon has been found at Craig Phadrig, near Inverness) and that enamelled objects with patterns similar to those found on the hanging bowls were produced in both Ireland and Scotland. Finds of raw material in English contexts (including glass rods used in the manufacture of *millefiori* enamel found in the excavations at the monasteries of Whitby and Jarrow) show that there was a capability for the manufacture of objects decorated with such designs in England. Whether this type of enamelling was representative of a British sub-culture of Anglo-Saxon art or whether it was re-introduced into England in, say, the late sixth century is unclear. It is, however, likely that, at the time when Christianity was introduced into Anglo-Saxon England, there was a region, made up of north-west England, Northumbria, Ireland and Scotland, which had a common stylistic tradition based on the developed spiral ornament. The same tradition is also seen dimly in Wales. The ornamental style was clearly well established in these areas before the motifs were used in the Durham Gospel fragment A.II.10 and the Book of Durrow. It would be reasonable to assume that the taste for spiral ornament was already present in the English mind before the Conversion and that the influence of the Irish Church, so clearly seen in the historical record, encouraged the scribe to use such motifs in the newly introduced manuscript art. The popularity of the spiral motif in the Christian art of England is undoubted. It appears not only in metalwork and in the pages of manuscripts, but also in sculpture, and does not disappear from the Anglo-Saxon repertoire until the end of the eighth century (cf. the Stockholm *Codex Aureus* and the Vespasian Psalter).

Such a summary will appear to most specialists to over-simplify and even to trivialize the problems of the spiral style. But in view of the amount of ink – sometimes amounting almost to blood – which has been spilt in discussing this subject in the last half century, it is impossible to rehearse here any of the detailed discussion put forward by scholars (some more chauvinistic than others) to argue a particular point. I believe that a consensus would generally agree with the statement made in the previous paragraph, but I do not deny the difficulty others might have in accepting it. There is a clear indication that the Northumbrian artistic tradition owed much to the Celtic world and we have seen some evidence of this transmission in the manuscript art, particularly an undoubted Irish element stemming from the Cathach and its now missing relations.

Pictish and Scottish elements

The art of the Picts – people who at the beginning of the seventh century were living in much of Scotland and particularly in the north and east, where their sculptured monuments survive – has long been related by scholars to the art of the great Gospel Books, although much of the discussion of these influences was undertaken in a period when the books themselves were seen to be Irish, or to owe everything to Ireland. The Picts had a stone sculptural tradition which developed over two or three centuries, and related motifs are also seen occasionally on metal objects. No Pictish manuscript art survives. The stone sculptural tradition, which may have tenuous relations with Romano-British art but which is unique unto itself, is seen in its initial form on what are known as Class I monuments. The content of the art consists of a number of

140

138 Cross-slab in the churchyard at
Aberlemno, Forfar.
Height 2.3 m

139 Pictish stone of Class II, from Hilton-of-Cadboll, Ross-shire. Height 2.46 m. (Edinburgh, National Museum of Antiquities of Scotland)

140 Pictish stone of Class I, at Dunnichen, Angus. Height 1.42 m

characteristic symbols which have been interpreted as memorial pictograms recording a person's relationship to a family or social group. Typically the symbols were carved on rough stone slabs or boulders. Among the symbols are animals which are clearly related in form to the Evangelist symbols of the Book of Durrow and the Echternach Gospels. A diagnostic feature in both media is the scrolled hips of the animals (be they bulls, eagles, geese or deer). Their obvious parallels have produced two alternative theories. Isabel Henderson has proposed that one Anglo-Saxon scribe coarsened the Pictish creatures and that the Evangelist symbols had their direct origin in the corpus of Pictish stone sculpture. Robert Stevenson, however, has put the opposite view that the animal art of Pictland derived from the manuscripts of Northumbria. The problem is complicated by the lack of any fixed chronology for the Pictish sculptures and by the fact that no exact prototype has been found for the Durrow/Pictish scroll pattern. On balance Stevenson is probably correct or, as I have attempted to demonstrate, there is a clear sequence in the animal art from the Germanic tradition of Sutton Hoo to the Book of Durrow and beyond and there is no earlier Pictish animal art of this sort. Further, as Stevenson points out, there is a great deal of scroll work in manuscript art, used in the most unlikely places (the wing of the St Matthew symbol in the Lindisfarne Gospels, for example). Other detailed arguments support this view and can only lead to the conclusion that the Pictish artists adopted at least the details of this style at some stage late in the seventh century. The Picts in a number of cases were quick to adopt external influences, from Mediterranean traditions for instance.

The contact between Pictland and Northumbria is brought into sharp relief by Bede's contemporary account (c.710) of a mission sent by Nechtan, the king of the Picts, to the monastery of Jarrow, asking ecclesiastical advice to do with the date of Easter and the form of the tonsure, but also asking for 'builders to be sent to build a church of stone in their country after the Roman fashion'. Bede records that the builders were sent to Pictland. This turning to the south by the Picts may be but one example of other similar requests. There is good cause to see this record as an indicator of the reason for the presence of clear Northumbrian stylistic traits in the Class II cross-slabs of the Picts, which are carefully dressed and on one face decorated with a carefully executed cross, and with various other motifs including animals, interlace and plant-scrolls. The free-standing cross was never used in the Pictish area and Isabel Henderson has therefore derived the form from the so-called 'pillow stones' (in effect grave markers) found in northern Northumbria. Such an origin is hard to justify and it seems more likely that the idea was either transferred from manuscript carpet-pages or from the free-standing cross (in the manner which we later encounter in the Isle of Man). The overall pattern is distinctly in the taste of the Northumbrians and many of the motifs (the animals on the side panels of the front of the Aberlemno churchyard stone, for example) are easily paralleled in Anglo-Saxon art. Similarly, the plant-scrolls seen on the Hilton-of-Cadboll stone and on fourteen other Pictish stones are clearly derived from eighth-century English sculpture, manuscripts and ivory carving. The symbols of the Class I stones are still encountered (as on the Hilton-of-Cadboll stone) and the eclectic nature of Pictish art at this period is clearly seen in other aspects of the sculpture which need not be considered here – in, for example, the great battle scenes and hunting scenes derived from Mediterranean sources, the origins of which are at least as complicated as the origins of the iconography of the Franks Casket (pp. 85–6).

Another group of material – metalwork – also illustrates the Anglo-Saxon influence on Pictish art. This was particularly emphasized by the find in 1958 of a major Pictish treasure on St Ninian's Isle, off the mainland of Shetland. This hoard, which dates from the eighth century, and which may well have been deposited in the face of a threatened Viking attack, consists of a group of penannular brooches, bowls and other objects (twenty-eight in all) made of silver, all but one (a silver hanging-bowl) of which appear to have been made in the Pictish area. The form of the brooches is Pictish and the art displays many aspects of a common Celtic style of interlaced ribbon ornament which is found also in Ireland, but which also has close relations with cast interlaced ribbon work found in Anglo-Saxon England. The animal ornament is closely related to that found in such manuscripts as the Barberini Gospels and, even earlier, in the Lindisfarne Gospels. There is in the art of the hoard a

141 'Pillow stone' (grave marker), from Hartlepool. Height 28.5 cm. (Durham Cathedral)

141

138

139

142, 143

117

considerable non-Anglo-Saxon element which may have come from Ireland or through Northumbria, but the strength of the Anglo-Saxon influence (as elsewhere in the sparse Pictish metalwork) is clear. It is perhaps best emphasized by the parallels which may be drawn between the animal head at the terminal of a mount with a runic incription, almost certainly from Northumbria, but found in the Thames, the animal head on the Anglo-Saxon helmet from York and the animal heads on one of the two chapes from the St Ninian's treasure.

Lothian, the Borders and Dumfriesshire were taken into the Northumbrian kingdom between 625 and 650 and sculptured crosses, of which that from Ruthwell is the most remarkable, were produced there in full Anglo-Saxon style until the end of the ninth century. But it was in the west at Iona that Anglo-Saxon, Irish and Pictish motifs met and produced an art seen on the sculptured crosses. The standing cross presumably had its origin in the Anglo-Saxon area and here developed the ringed head which was to be transported back to England in the Anglo-Danish period. The most complete surviving example of such a cross, dated perhaps c.800, is to be seen at Kildalton in Islay; but it is Iona which has produced the most important group of stone crosses, of which the most splendid, the St John's Cross, is now only a shattered wreck, reproduced in facsimile on the site. The St Martin's Cross has one face competently executed in the Pictish boss style and the other face historiated in a rather primitive fashion, very different from the highly sophisticated figural carving of Northumbria. The central panel encloses a Virgin and Child surrounded by four angels; other scenes include Samuel and David, David and his musicians and Abraham's sacrifice of Isaac. The ends of the cross arms were originally elongated by the use of a fillet of wood set in a mortice in each arm. Usually taken as the latest of the early group of Iona crosses (there are later cross slabs, from the Viking Age for example), it is usually dated to the late eighth or early ninth century. It is sometimes said that such figural scenes as are found here and on other cross slabs at Iona and on other sites in western Scotland are derived from Northumbrian prototypes. This assertion has been

64
144

137

145
146

142, 143 Analytic and expanded drawings to show animal ornament on a pommel from St Ninian's Isle, Shetland

144 *Right*: chape from the treasure found on St Ninian's Isle, Shetland. Width 8.2 cm. (Edinburgh, National Museum of Antiquities of Scotland)

questioned because about this time (in the early ninth century) crosses with fairly sophisticated iconographic cycles were being produced in Ireland at, for example, Kells, a monastery founded (or refounded) by monks from Iona in the first decade of the ninth century. Attempts have consequently been made to derive the Iona sculptural tradition from Ireland; chronologically, however, this is difficult to accept, rather it must be the other way round. Although the figural cycles on the St Martin's Cross and on the other Iona sculptures may not be drawn from Northumbria (they are likely to have come from Pictland), the crosses themselves must be of Northumbrian inspiration. The Irish crosses are thus derived at second hand from those of England.

147 *Left*: detail of the opening word (*Liber*) of St Matthew's Gospel, from the Book of Kells (Dublin, Trinity College, A.I.6(58), fol. 29r). 33 × 25 cm. See p. 129

148 *Right*: portrait of Christ, from the Book of Kells (Dublin, Trinity College, A.I.6(58), fol. 32v). 33 × 25 cm. See p. 129

The Irish dimension

There is in Irish sculpture very little ornament derived directly from England, but a few motifs must come from England, as, for example, the plant-scroll on the South Cross at Clonmacnoise and on the Tower Cross at Kells and interlaced animals which occur on a small number of crosses. It is, however, in the Irish metalwork that most Anglo-Saxon influence is to be seen. About the year 700 two magnificent objects were produced in Ireland which are technically as superb as any metal objects found in contemporary Europe – the Ardagh Chalice and the so-called 'Tara' Brooch. To these can now be added the chalice and paten recently found at Derrynaflan, Co. Tipperary, the former of which is, however, perhaps later and rather less technically competent than that from Ardagh. The Ardagh Chalice is of silver and is embellished below the rim with a girdle of panels containing enamelled studs, panels of impressed silver and openwork panels containing animal designs executed in gold filigree on openwork impressed sheets. Similar panels are applied to the foot of the chalice. The stem consists of a cast cylinder decorated with chip-carving. The handles of the chalice are cast and inlaid with plates and studs. An inscription recording the names of the Apostles is lightly incised on the body of the chalice, as is a group of animal heads. Much of the ornament of the chalice has its roots

151

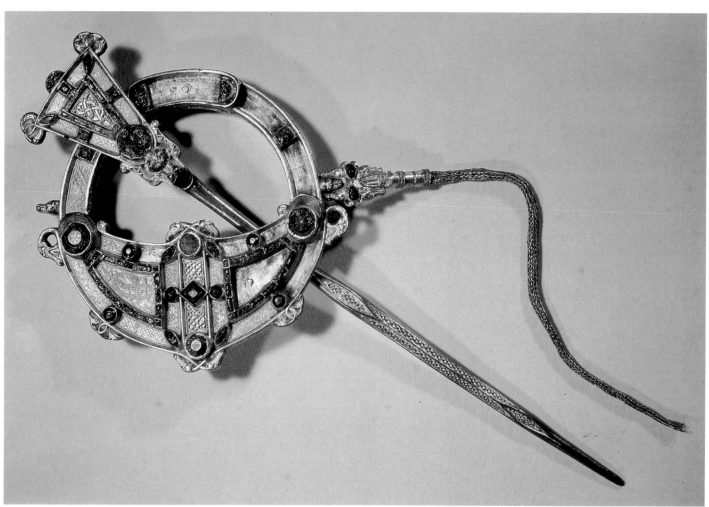

149 Brooch found at Hunterston, Ayrshire.
Height 12.2 cm (Edinburgh, National Museum of Antiquities of Scotland).
See p. 129

150 The Tara Brooch.
Length of pin 22.5 cm (Dublin, National Museum of Ireland).
See p. 129

151 The Ardagh Chalice.
Height 15 cm (Dublin, National Museum of Ireland).
See p. 128

IN PRIN CIPIO

152 'In Principio', the beginning of St John's Gospel, from the Bible of Charles the Bald (Paris, Bibliothèque Nationale, lat.2, fol. 11r). See p. 133

153 Opening of St Matthew's Gospel, from the Saint-Martin-des-Champs Gospels (Paris, Bibliothèque de l'Arsenal, 599, fol. 16r). 26.5 × 19 cm. See p. 133

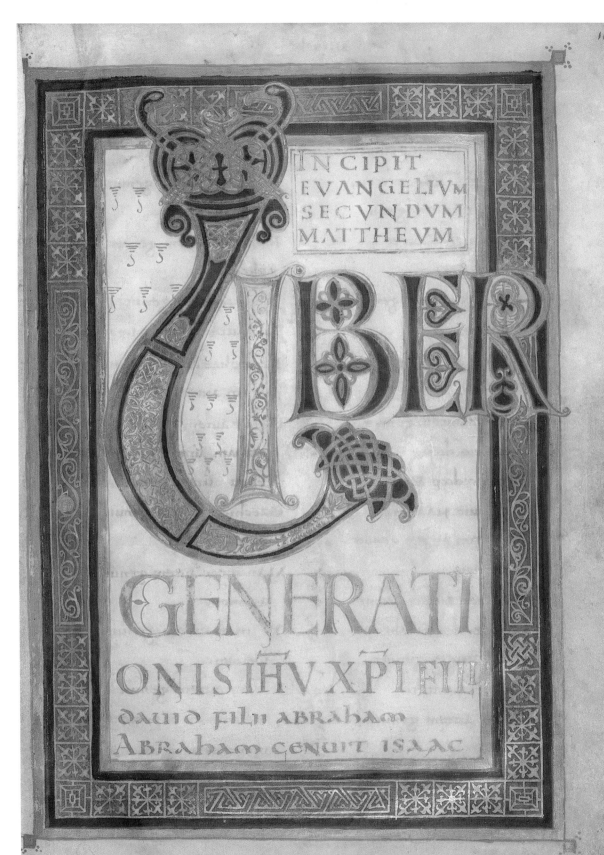

INCIPIT
EVANGELIVM
SECVNDVM
MATTHEVM

LIBER

GENERATI
ONIS IHV XPI FILI
dauid filii abraham
Abraham genuit isaac

154 St Matthew, from the Trier Gospels, probably painted at Echternach (Trier, Cathedral Treasury, Codex 61, fol. 18v). 30 × 24.5 cm. See p. 131

155 Evangelist, from the Maaseik Gospel fragment (Maaseik, treasury of the church of St Catherine). 24.4 × 18.3 cm. See p. 131

156 Portable altar from the Abbey of
Adelhausen, near Freiburg im Breisgau
(Freiburg im Breisgau,
Augustinermuseum). Length 37.7 cm.
See p. 137.

in Irish art – the enamelled studs and the special ornament can be paralleled at an earlier date – but a good deal of the immediate inspiration must come from Anglo-Saxon ornament, partly from metalwork, partly from manuscripts. The cloisonné plaques on the handle, for instance, are derived from English models (prototypes can be seen, for example, on the Sutton Hoo jewellery), whilst the animal ornament in filigree is also close in technique and form to English parallels; the interlace presumably also came from Anglo-Saxon sources. The Anglo-Saxon tradition is a powerful element in this art but it was the eclectic genius of Irish craftsmen which brought together a grammar of ornament to produce some of the finest pieces of jewellery and plate ever made.

The Anglo-Saxon elements seen here are most frequently encountered on the pseudo-penannular or penannular brooches commonly found in Ireland, the most important example of which is the Tara Brooch (actually found at 150 Bettystown, Co. Meath). This is in every way as competent a piece of craftsmanship as the Ardagh Chalice, has many of the same features and was presumably made at the same time. Robert Stevenson has made a good case, however, for the priority of the brooch from Hunterston, Ayrshire, which, 149 while not perhaps of as high quality as the Tara Brooch, is closely parallel in technique and form. It was perhaps made in the west of Scotland and, like the Tara Brooch and the Ardagh Chalice, has close stylistic connections with Northumbria. It seems clear, however, that in Scotland and Ireland, during the years around 700, art was to a great extent drawing on Anglo-Saxon stylistic elements to create the special expression of style which was to flower later in the century in the St Ninian's Isle treasure and in the Book of Kells.

The Book of Kells (Dublin, Trinity College, A.I.6(58)) is undoubtedly the most ostentatious book to survive from the early medieval period. It measures 33 × 25 cm and is illuminated with abandon in a profusion of colours, blue, greenish blue and brownish purple being dominant. It has ten pages of illuminated canon tables and five pages with Evangelist symbols, which may represent author portraits, as each of the four Gospels is also preceded by a page decorated with all four symbols. There is also a 'portrait' of Christ and 148 one carpet page. Each Gospel has a great monogram, as has folio 29, where the 147 L of Liber is similarly treated. There are numerous initials of varying size scattered through the text, as well as a number of miniatures. The effect is overwhelming, almost vulgar in its totally baroque ornament; here is the apogee of insular art, in a book that has been studied and commented on since the days of Giraldus Cambrensis in the late twelfth century.

Its origins have been much discussed; it was probably at Kells after the beginning of the ninth century (although there is no real hint of its presence there until the eleventh century) but was almost certainly not produced there. After a few years when a Pictish origin for the manuscript was adumbrated, the most favoured origin would now seem to be Iona at some date shortly before the evacuation of that monastery to Kells in the early years of the ninth century (i.e. in the late eighth century). The ornament of the manuscript draws on many sources, Scottish, Pictish, continental, possibly even Byzantine, as well as Anglo-Saxon. It is eclectic and innovative. It had little, if any, effect on Anglo-Saxon art but drew certain ornamental details (either directly or indirectly) from Anglo-Saxon sources. These English elements are clear – animal ornament, interlace, step patterns in imitation of metalwork cells, 'potted plants' and traces (but no more than traces) of plant-scrolls. The colour ranges link it with the Lichfield Gospels, in ornament it runs the whole gamut of manuscript and metalwork art, while in its text and make-up it goes back to the traditions of the Book of Durrow. It is unique, *sui generis*, puzzling and one of the greatest productions of the early medieval period.

Irish art of the period 675–800 is seen at its most supreme in the metalwork. The Tara Brooch and the Ardagh Chalice are brilliant technical achievements. Irish sculpture in this early period, on the other hand, lacks originality and has less technical quality than that from Scotland and England and, if we accept that the Book of Kells was not painted in Ireland, it is clear that there is little quality in the surviving Irish manuscripts. It is probable that only a portion of the original corpus survives, but generally Ireland was a receiver and not a donor at this period and, although technically the metalwork was of high quality, the motifs used were largely derivative. Only the developed spiral, common to much of the north and west of the British Isles, was received with any eagerness into English art, where it may indeed already have been present. The persistent tradition that Ireland was the inspiration for much insular art of the seventh and eighth century must be seen then in this perspective.

Irish art of the ninth century loses the quality of its precursors; only in sculpture is there any development. Anglo-Saxon influence trickled continuously into the metalwork but in all other areas the art depended on its roots in Ireland. There are few if any English imports in Ireland of this period and not until long after the Scandinavian settlements became firmly established in the late tenth century did Irish art open itself more thoroughly to outside influences and transmit anything to England.

England and the Continent

The origins of the first Anglo-Saxon manuscripts in both Ireland and on the Continent have been mentioned above (pp. 29–32). The sources of the ornament have been seen as English, British, Irish and Germanic, with traces in the carpet pages, the Evangelist portraits and their symbols of Mediterranean and Eastern influences. Throughout the period covered by this book there was continuous contact between the Church in England and the more established Churches of Gaul and Italy and an irregular, second-hand contact with the eastern Church based on Byzantium.

But England was also a donor. As missionaries travelled to the Continent – to Frisia and Germany for example – and sent books home for service and study, so English taste spread abroad. St Boniface, the English founder of the Church in Frisia and northern Germany, was always begging for books and his letters are full of requests for, and gifts of, books; thus in a letter to Archbishop Egbert of York, he writes (*c*.747):

> Have copied and sent to me, I pray you, some of the treatises of Bede, whom, we are told, God endowed with spiritual understanding and allowed to shine in your midst. We would also like to enjoy the light God bestowed on you. Meanwhile, I send you as a token of affection a copy of the letters of St Gregory, which I have received from Rome, and which, so far as I know, have not yet reached Britain. If you wish, I will send more, for I have many from the same source.

Other missionaries, Lul for example, wrote in similar vein, although nobody was quite so openly demanding as Boniface. But it was not only missionaries who sought books from England. The great teacher Alcuin, who was called as a man of distinction from York to the court of Charlemagne, was not above asking for scholarly facilities. As befits an academic *prima donna*, his style is more convoluted:

> I, your Flaccus, according to your exhortation and encouragement, am occupied in supplying to some under the roof of St Martin the honey of the sacred Scriptures; am eager to inebriate others with the old wine of ancient learning; begin to nourish others on the fruits of grammatical subtlety; long to illumine some with the order of the stars, like the painted ceiling of a great man's house; becoming many things to many men, that I may instruct many to the profit of the Holy Church of God and to the adornment of your imperial kingdom, that the grace of the Almighty be not void in me, nor the bestowal of your bounty in vain.
>
> But I, your servant, miss to some extent the rarer books of scholastic learning which I had in my own country through the excellent and devoted zeal of my master and also through some toil of my own. I tell these things to your Excellency, in case it may perchance be agreeable to your counsel, which is most eager for the whole of knowledge, that I send some of our pupils to choose there what we need, and to bring into France the flowers of Britain; that not in York only there may be a 'garden enclosed', but in Tours the 'plants of Paradise with the fruit of the orchard'.

It was thus that English books were brought to the Continent or copied for continental monasteries. Three of Boniface's books survive in Fulda, one an Italian book which had been bound in Northumbria, another an insular Gospel Book (the Cadmug Gospels) and the third a book of French origin. It was perhaps thus that the Echternach Gospels may have reached the monastery of Echternach, founded by the English St Willibrord (658–739) in 698. It is possible, for example, that the Leningrad Gospels reached France (where it was until the eighteenth century) as a gift of exchange soon after it was written.

The English style of manuscript illumination caught on abroad, so much so that it is sometimes difficult to decide whether a book was written on the Continent or in England. Such a manuscript is the Maaseik Gospel fragment (in the treasury of the church of St Catherine), which has been ascribed by Nordenfalk to York, but which other scholars (Lowe, Wright and Budny) see as painted on the Continent, perhaps at Echternach. Another book probably painted at Echternach – the Trier Gospels (Trier, Cathedral Treasury, Codex 61) – also has many insular traits. It was written and painted in the middle of the eighth century by two scribes, one of whom had an Anglo-Saxon hand and signed his name 'Thomas'; the other scribe wrote in French uncial. The insular elements, as seen in the St Matthew portrait illustrated here, are obvious: the interlacing, the barred chair and the treatment of the clothes are all features encountered in English manuscripts. Thomas, however, signs one of the pages of canon tables and this is as continental a design as one is likely to find: only at the base of the capitals are there fret patterns which would be at home in an insular milieu. There can be little doubt that the Trier Gospels was copied from two sources – an insular Gospel Book (but not the Echternach Gospels) and (for the canon tables) a sixth- or seventh-century Italian manuscript.

Anglo-Saxon art provided ornamental inspiration to continental artists. From Italian and Byzantine sources portraiture and realism could be introduced, but the brilliant jewel-like quality of English art was apparently highly desirable and, as has been shown, even before Charlemagne came to the throne, motifs such as interlaced ribbon ornament were making themselves felt in continental *scriptoria*. The influence is most clearly seen in north-east France, where a Franco-Saxon school developed in places like Saint-Amand;

155

154

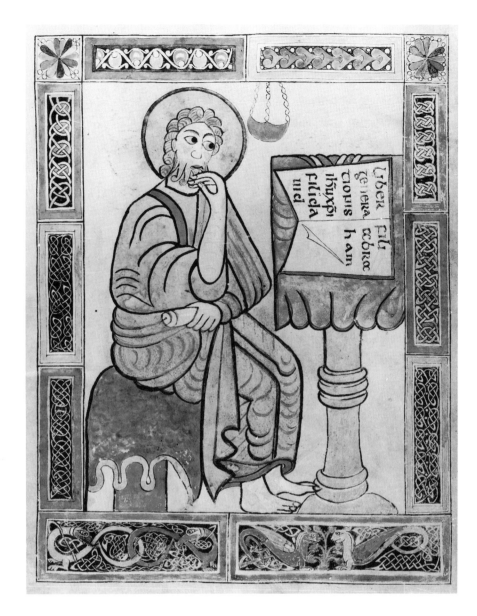

157 St Matthew, from the Cutbercht
Gospels
(Vienna, Nationalbibliothek, Cod.
1224, fol. 17v). 31 × 24 cm

the poverty-stricken painting of the Merovingian monasteries was ripe for a
development which reached its peak in the reign of Charlemagne.

The Court school of Charlemagne produced two groups of manuscripts; the
first, the Palace school, was inspired almost completely by Italian and
Byzantine models. With an economy of line and a spontaneity of ornament
they produced manuscripts in a pure classical – even Hellenistic – tradition,
free from tight ornament and ornate embellishment. The tradition which is
seen here did not die out with the collapse of the Carolingian polity, but
survived in the school of Reims, of which the Utrecht Psalter is a major
representative and one that, as is shown below, had a considerable influence
on English art of the tenth century, as it was to have on the art of the whole of
northern France and Germany.

The second group of manuscripts of the court of Charlemagne of the years
before and after his coronation in 800 is known as the Ada school, after the
reference to a man called Ada in one of the nine manuscripts which form this

229

group. These manuscripts are rich and highly decorated and one of them, the Saint-Martin-des-Champs Gospels (Paris, Bibliothèque de l'Arsenal, 599), which dates from the late eighth century, will serve to illustrate their insular influences. The page illustrated shows the great initial from the beginning of St 153 Matthew's Gospel. The interlace ornament has obvious Anglo-Saxon origins, but as it is examined in greater detail it becomes clear that there are other insular elements; the cloisonné pattern in each corner, for example, the plant-scroll in the border and the fret pattern at top and bottom. This was an ornamental tradition which was to continue for many years, long after Charlemagne's death in 814. Charlemagne was the inspirer and the patron of this art, partly through the advice he received from the shrewd politician and ecclesiastic, Alcuin, whom he had brought from England; a man described by the Emperor's biographer, Einhard, as 'the most learned man of the day'.

Alcuin was head of the Abbey of Tours from 796 to 804 and was succeeded by another Anglo-Saxon, Fridugisus, who was abbot from 804 to 834. Tours was the great centre of French learning for practically the whole of the ninth century and the production centre, with its satellites, of many of the great books of the period, books which were distributed to courts and monasteries throughout the northern empire. More than sixty illuminated books still survive from the ninth-century Tours *scriptorium* (none from Tours itself, as the library was burnt in a Norse attack). In the early years of the century under Alcuin and Fridugisus there was a considerable Anglo-Saxon influence at Tours and the manuscripts display many insular ornamental traits. A fragmentary Bible of this school (Paris, Bibliothèque Nationale, lat.8847) even bears interlaced bird ornament in the pillars and arches of its canon tables in direct descent from a Northumbrian prototype. But the Tours *scriptorium* was more influenced by a number of Roman books, which produced a pictorial painterly style, more three-dimensional than that of Reims, that reaches its heights in the Vivian Bible and the Lothar Gospels, with their great dedication paintings based on Late Antique models. Anglo-Saxon influence can still be traced in these manuscripts, but the real Anglo-Saxon influence of the ninth century is to be seen in the manuscripts painted in the north of France, where the so-called Franco-Saxon school built on Northumbrian traditions.

This is the best seen in the second Bible of Charles the Bald (Paris, Bibliothèque Nationale, lat.2), in which there are seventy-four large and splendidly intricate initials of which that illustrated shows in its interlace, in its 152 animal heads and in many of its small details, traces of English influence. This manuscript was probably produced at Saint-Amand between 871 and 877 at a time when we have little evidence of such splendid books in England. The style continues into the tenth and eleventh century in such manuscripts as the Arsenal Gospels (Paris, Bibliothèque de l'Arsenal, 592).

The Cutbercht Gospels and the Tassilo Chalice

Another area of Anglo-Saxon influence was Bavaria and western Austria, where traditions drawn from England and Italy produced an art which has a distinctive character, particularly in metalwork. Manuscript influences can also be traced here. Indeed one manuscript, known after its Anglo-Saxon scribe, Cutbercht (Vienna, Nationalbibliothek, Cod. 1224), is completely 157 insular in its ornament and script and was probably produced in the diocese of Salzburg. In the parish church of Bischofshofen, not far from Salzburg, is the

158 The Rupertus Cross, from the
parish church of Bischofshofen, near
Salzburg.
Height 1.58 m

159 The Ormside Bowl
Diameter 13.8 cm. See also pls. 56, 57.
(York, the Yorkshire Museum)

158   so-called Rupertus Cross, of gilt bronze impressed sheet set on a wooden core
and embellished with glass studs. It is 1.58 m high and was either a memorial
cross, a hanging cross or an altar cross without a foot. The ornament is closely
159   related to that of the Ormside Bowl, although more stylized in that the plant-
scroll develops into animals as on the Witham Pins rather than being
inhabited. The glass studs in dark blue and white are much larger than any
found in insular contexts; precise technical parallels are lacking in the British
Isles, but the motif is certainly English in taste. It is impossible to say with any
certainty whether it was made in England or in Austria; the style and
inspiration of the ornament is Anglo-Saxon. In view of its size it seems

134

probable that, like the Cutbercht Gospels, it was made on the Continent either by an Englishman or by somebody trained in the English tradition. That there were English craftsmen working on the Continent is attested by the *Liber Pontificalis* ('The Book of the Popes'), which clearly states that craftsmen from the *Schola Saxonum* in Rome were making plate for the altar of St Peter's itself – an indication of the high regard in which English craftsmen were held.

We have seen that a fair number of English objects have been found on the Continent – the Franks Casket, the Fulda bookbinding and the Gandersheim Casket among them; others come from as far away as Paris and Bologna. These objects taken by pilgrims or missionaries appear to have established a taste for Anglo-Saxon minor arts to such an extent that a distinct school of metalwork, the Anglo-Carolingian school, grew up within the empire, based in its designs on eighth-century English art. The most important object (but not the grandest) is the Tassilo Chalice, so called because of an inscription round the foot, TASSILO DVX FORTIS LIVTPIRC VIRGA REGALIS, which refers to Tassilo, Duke of Bavaria and his wife, Liutpirc, daughter of the Langobard king Desiderius. Tassilo reigned from 748 to his deposition by Charlemagne in 788; as the chalice is probably a foundation present to the monastery of Kremsmünster (where it is still preserved), it must date between 777 (when the monastery was founded) and 788 (when Tassilo was deposed).

161

160 Christ, from the Montpellier Psalter (Montpellier, Bibliothèque de l'université, 409, fol. 2v). 32 × 22 cm

161 The Tassilo Chalice. Height 25.5 cm. (Kremsmünster Abbey, Austria)

135

162, 163 *Above and opposite*: two details of the ornament on the Tassilo Chalice

The chalice is large, nearly 27 cm high with a capacity in its cup of 1.75 litres. It is made of gilded copper in two pieces: first, the cup and, second, the foot, which is cast together with the knop. Silver plates ornamented with niello inlay were applied to the surface. The chalice has been the subject of a seminal study by Günther Haseloff who has shown that the portraits of Christ and the Evangelists, with their symbols in the main fields of the cup and four portraits of more obscure or even unidentified personalities on the foot of the chalice, stand in a close relation to the insular-influenced manuscripts of the Salzburg region and particularly the Montpellier Psalter (Montpellier, Bibliothèque de l'université, 409), which was produced at Mondsee before 778. The rest of the surface of the chalice is decorated with animal and plant ornament executed in deep chip-carving in a style very close to that found in the eighth century in England (cf. pl. 66). The main stylistic difference between the English and continental animals are the spread back legs of the latter.

The animal style of the Tassilo Chalice recurs on secular metalwork found from Yugoslavia to Norway. It is particularly common in Holland and northern Germany where it occurs on strap-ends, belt-slides, spurs and other objects of personal jewellery, as for example a pair of ear-rings. Two silver cups, one from Fejö in Denmark and the other from Pettstadt in south Germany, and the great bookbinding from Lindau (New York, Pierpont Morgan Library, M.1) demonstrate its popularity with wealthy patrons. The style seems to have died out in the course of the ninth century although a

160

162, 163

related, discrete, successor is perhaps that found on two candlesticks from the monastery of Kremsmünster and on a small group of enamelled brooches of south German or Austrian provenance.

Related to the animal ornament of the Tassilo Chalice is a small body of stone sculpture which is associated with the same insular influences on the Continent. The stones come from the church of St Johann, Mustair, Switzerland. The animals are caught up in an irregular interlace, and although they are undoubtedly influenced by Anglo-Saxon ornament may well, because of the highly irregular nature of the ribbon interlace, belong to a very late phase of such influence, perhaps in the late ninth century.

An entirely different form of insular influence on the Continent is seen on a small portable altar from the monastery of Adelhausen, near Freiburg. The altar is only 38 cm long and has a central porphyry panel surrounded by silver plates and enamelled ornament. The insular influence is evident in the interlace ornament chased, nielloed and parcel-gilded on the plates, which flank the porphyry central panel. This type of interlace and technique is rare, but it is paralleled on a pair of equal-armed brooches from a late ninth-century hoard found at Slagveld, near Muysen, Brabant, Belgium (themselves paralleled by a fragment of a similar brooch found in Denmark). The pattern must be derived from manuscript sources as it has little in common with English metalworking techniques.

Throughout the manuscripts and minor arts of this period in northern Europe traces of insular ornament can be seen. The Adelhausen altar with its

164 Analysis of ornament on the Tassilo Chalice

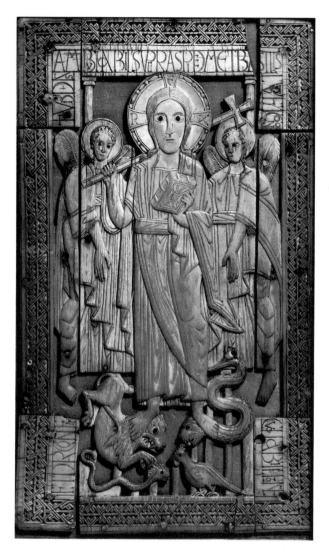

165, 166 Two ivory plaques from the church of St Martin, Genoels-Elderen. Both 30 × 18 cm. (Brussels, Musées Royaux d'Art et d'Histoire)

continental enamelling is paralleled in its interlace patterns by the two ivory plaques (sometimes actually identified as English) from the church of St Martin, Genoels-Elderen (now in Brussels), which frame scenes of Mediterranean origin (Christ treading on the serpents, the Visitation and the Annunciation). The court art of Charlemagne provides glimpses of high insular tradition and has pale reflections in provincial centres like Fleury, where delicate interlace is, for example, seen in a Book of the Prophets (Orléans, Bibliothèque municipale, 17). Anglo-Saxon art, strong and vital, penetrated much of northern Europe.

England and Scandinavia

Strangely enough, Anglo-Saxon art had little effect on the art of Scandinavia before the tenth century, despite persistent attempts by Scandinavian specialists to identify English and Irish influence in eighth- and ninth-century Scandinavia. Anglo-Carolingian art flourished in south Scandinavia for a short time (it is sometimes denominated as Style F), but, despite the constant contacts across the North Sea during the ninth century and despite the fairly substantial body of insular material found in Scandinavia taken there as a

138

167 Brooch from Austris, Gotland, Sweden. Diameter 9.8 cm. (Stockholm, Statens Historiska Museum)

result of the Viking raids, the art of the North remained relatively untouched by English influence. One exception is provided by a group of brooches from eastern Sweden, of which the example from Austris, Gotland, is the finest example. Here can be seen, nielloed in the silver, speckled animal ornament. The animals have rather untidily interlaced limbs, spiral hips and amorphous heads. The technique is undoubtedly derived from the Trewhiddle style, but is perhaps closer in stylistic detail to the ornament seen on the shrine-plate in the British Museum discussed below (p. 145), which has itself in part a Scandinavian inspiration. It is also possible that the granulation technique (clustered globules of gold soldered together) found on this brooch may be derived from Britain, as it is seen, for example, on the Alfred Jewel.

England then in the eighth and ninth centuries had an important influence on European art. Never again was it to have this tremendous impact. In the centuries which follow, it gave to Europe in a much more limited fashion – particularly to Normandy, as we shall see, through the medium of manuscripts. The influence of missionaries and scholars dwindled and the churches and courts of France and Germany became more self-confident; only in the provinces immediately bordering the North Sea is any real English influence to be seen.

167

121, 122

5 From Alfred to the Conquest

LINKS BETWEEN the art of the tenth century and that of the preceding centuries are difficult to decipher. In some respects this is not surprising in that the ninth century (and particularly the late ninth century) was a period of trauma in England. The Scandinavian attack on Lindisfarne in 793 ushered in a period of raids on exposed and vulnerable monasteries and trading stations along the English coast. The raids were sporadic at first, but towards the middle of the ninth century they became bolder and more organized. A Danish army wintered in England in 854, but it was not until 865 that the raids changed their character and settlement began to be the aim of the Scandinavians, who soon established their authority over much of the north and east of England. By 879 the Scandinavians were recognized as rulers of the whole region north of a line drawn between the rivers Lee and Dee. They consolidated their newly-won territory, brought additional land into cultivation, broke up the great ecclesiastical estates like those which had belonged to Lindisfarne, fortified towns, adopted the Christian religion and, through the influence of the Church, started to become English.

The political scene was not, however, quiescent; a new element was introduced in about 900, when Scandinavians from Norway and the west of the British Isles settled in Cheshire, Lancashire, Westmorland and Cumberland. At the same time the rulers of the Scandinavian kingdoms came under severe military and political pressure from the English kings of Wessex; first from Alfred, then from Edward the Elder, and then Athelstan, as well as from the formidable Æthelflæd, Lady of the Mercians (Alfred's daughter). By 954 the English had established political control over the erstwhile Danelaw. The Scandinavians remained, anglicized landowners; the old order had changed, monasteries had disappeared, the land had been redistributed, towns redeveloped and the ancient kingdoms were absorbed under one English ruler.

Writing in the middle of this traumatic period, King Alfred woefully described the state of learning in England:

> So completely had learning decayed in England that there were few men on this side of the Humber who could apprehend their services in English or even translate a letter from Latin into English and I think that there were not many beyond the Humber. There were so few of them that I cannot recollect a single one south of the Thames when I succeeded to the kingdom. Thanks be to God Almighty that we now have provision for teachers.

There is necessarily a certain homiletic exaggeration in this passage: the picture cannot have been as grim as that painted by the king, the lamps of learning and of art continued (if with diminished vigour) to burn even in the darkest days. It is unlikely that there was any serious disruption of English life before the arrival of the great army in 865 and, after that date, trimmers both in

168 *Opposite*: Detail of a fragment of a cross-shaft from Newgate, York. (York, Yorkshire Museum)

141

169 Detail of the Gosforth Cross, Cumberland. See pl. 186

Church and state presumably feathered their own nest, employed craftsmen and artists and waited for better days to come. One must not, however, denigrate Alfred's serious sense of purpose and the success of his policy. He recruited scholars from many places: Asser, his biographer, came from Wales; Plegmund, archbishop of Canterbury, from Mercia; Grimbald came from Reims, and the abbot of his newly founded abbey of Athelney was a certain John who came from Saxony. The recovery of art and learning in the tenth century was certainly in part due to Alfred's inspiration and planning. The unity of England under Alfred was built on very shaky foundations; to most Englishmen loyalty to the family group or the petty lord over-rode a national vision. None the less there are indications of an upturn in the cultural life of the country (although the evidence is uneven because of the selective survival of documents and monuments). After the Canterbury Bible no major illuminated manuscript is known until well on into the tenth century. The metalwork tradition is misty. The presence, however, of a brilliant school of embroidery (testified by the stole, girdle and maniple from St Cuthbert's shrine, made in   205–7
the early years of the tenth century) demonstrates a lushness and an innovatory brilliance in art just after Alfred's death in 900. The unanswerable question is whether innovation sprang from the self-conscious cultural revival of an egotistical and powerful Alfred, or whether the art was a continuation of the tradition of the early ninth century, taking into itself some aspects of the continental styles developed under Charlemagne and his successors. The seemingly innovatory element may have been merely the product of the disturbed times when churches were pillaged and books burnt.

Scandinavian art in England

One new element is, however, evident in the art of northern England. The new settlers brought with them Scandinavian taste, and many objects decorated in the Scandinavian styles have been found. Some were imported, either as trade goods or as articles brought in by immigrants, but some were made in this country. It is clear, for example, from a matrix found in York, that objects   171
were being manufactured which were ornamented in purely Scandinavian styles, made for sale to the new settlers. Finds of such patently Scandinavian objects as a chape decorated in the Borre/Jellinge overlap style are interesting   172
in that it is impossible to say whether they were manufactured in Scandinavia or England. Sometimes the two national styles unite: a strap-end from York,   170
for example, bears a version of a ring-chain ornament which is based on the ninth/tenth-century Borre style of Scandinavia and yet is clearly different from anything produced in that region.

The synthesis between English and Scandinavian art is best seen in the sculpture that survives in northern England. The Scandinavian settlers had produced little stone sculpture in their homelands but, when they encountered this medium in their new country, they avidly adopted it either as patrons or as practitioners of the art. Their interest in stone sculpture is clearly demonstrated by the extraordinary number of monuments produced by the settlers or their descendants in the north of England; there are fragments of more than five hundred sculptured stones of the tenth and eleventh centuries in Yorkshire alone.

The earliest Scandinavian style found in English contexts is the Borre style, named after a ship burial from a site of that name in the south-east of Norway.

170–72 Three finds from Yorkshire showing
Scandinavian art and its influence. *Left*: strap-end.
Length 4.9 cm. *Centre*: matrix. Height 4.7 cm. *Right*:
scabbard chape. Length 8.6 cm.
All save the chape are decorated in the Borre style – or
versions of it; the animal on the chape is more like the
Jellinge ribbon shaped animals. (York, Yorkshire
Museum)

One particular motif of this style, the ring-chain pattern, which is in effect a
balanced ribbon interlace, became very popular in the British Isles. It occurs in
Ireland, the Isle of Man and Scotland in a pure form. In England it appears in a
relatively pure form on the outstanding piece of Scandinavian stone sculpture,
169   the cross from Gosforth, Cumberland, and became reasonably popular in
various guises elsewhere in Cumbria, appearing, for example, at Rockcliff,
Beckermet St John, Crosscanonby, Waberthwaite and Muncaster. The style
was imitated elsewhere in England, as on the York strap-end mentioned
above, and in more elaborate form on a pendant from a necklace found in a
173   grave at Saffron Walden, Essex, which is closely related to a group of similar,
but rather simpler, roundels found throughout the south of England and
particularly East Anglia. The classic form of the Borre ring-chain is clearly
seen on English sculpture and a modified version was adapted by the
metalworkers. By definition it must date from after the first settlements of 876.
None of the other motifs which make up the style in Scandinavia are, however,
found in its English expression, although it is possible that the backward-
looking animals on certain disc-brooches from York and elsewhere may have
their origin in part in the Borre style.

The Jellinge style, named after the incised ornament on a silver cup found in
the Danish royal necropolis of that name, is more clearly seen in northern
England on a handful of stones. It rarely occurs on metal objects, although
degenerate – almost unrecognizable – elements of the style are occasionally
recognized in southern English silver. In Scandinavia the Jellinge style is
conventionally bracketed in date between the last quarter of the ninth century
and the late tenth century, and it would seem unlikely that it appears in

173 Pendant from a necklace found at
Saffron Walden, Essex.
Height 5.5 cm. (Saffron Walden
Museum)

174 An unfinished carving of a Jellinge style animal. Probably a reject from a stone-carver's workshop. Found at Coppergate, York. Height 22.3 cm. (York, Yorkshire Museum)

England much before 900. The best examples of objects decorated in this style are found on sculpture from York, which might well be the centre into which the style was first introduced. Perhaps the most interesting piece of York sculpture was a fragment excavated on the Coppergate site. It demonstrates many of the diagnostic features of animals of the Jellinge style – the double contour, ribbon-like body, spiral hip, lip lappet and pigtail. The legs and pigtail interlace with the body of the animal in a rather untidy fashion. This piece was unfinished, having apparently been discarded by the craftsman near the site of his workshop (a unique example of a waste product from a sculptor's atelier). Of much finer quality is the fragment of a cross-shaft from Newgate, York, which, though damaged, retains the remains of a finely carved frieze of three Jellinge beasts, each one being swallowed by its neighbour. Remains of paint on the surface hint at a much more fearsome original appearance.

York, the capital of a Scandinavian kingdom, has produced enough sculpture of Scandinavian taste to enable us to define a school. Recent excavations beneath the minster and finds like those from Coppergate and Newgate have revolutionized the study of the Scandinavian styles of northern England. For the first time the products of a metropolitan school have been properly identified in sufficient quantity to judge both quality and style. With a few exceptions – the Newgate Cross is one – the quality is coarse and unambitious and it is difficult to say whether the surviving material represents the highest possible achievement of the Anglo-Scandinavian sculptor or whether it is ordinary run-of-the-mill stuff. It seems as though the sculptors of this school never achieved, nor were interested in achieving, the quality of craftsmanship we have seen in certain eighth-century English carvings. Perhaps they did not have the skill, perhaps they did not have the taste, perhaps they did not care. It is just possible that the craftsmen relied for their ultimate finish on paint, which when applied might conceal the more obvious errors, infelicities and coarseness in design. The surviving products are generally miserable and slipshod, but the style is not without interest.

Its most interesting features probably comprise the zoomorphic forms best represented perhaps in the ornament of Shaft 1 from York Minster. James Lang has described the motif as a beast-chain: a good description as it consists of a series of interlocked Jellinge-style beasts caught up in an interlace of pigtails, tails and ribbons. The pattern is not regular and the animals vary in detail. Related motifs from York include birds set in a similar chain-like fashion and more degenerate versions of Jellinge-style birds and animals. The sculptors of York presumably influenced the art of the North and East Ridings of Yorkshire, for similar patterns are found elsewhere; a particularly fine example occurs further north on a shaft from Haughton-le-Skerne.

Some of the sculpture found outside the city is, however, of even poorer quality. In Ryedale, for example, a number of churches have produced cross-shafts which group together to form a school. The classic example of such sculpture is the cross-shaft from Middleton, often illustrated and discussed. The sagging animal on this shaft has the stylistic elements of Jellinge art, often distorted and misunderstood but just recognizable – the double contour, the irregular interlace, the (in this case very much misunderstood) lip-lappet, the pigtail and so on. Other stones from Sinnington, Ellerburn and Pickering were either carved by the same hand or belong to the same school. Other fragments

174

168

175

176

177

175–7 Animal ornament on (*left*) Shaft 1 from York
Minster; (*centre*) a cross-shaft at Haughton-le-Skerne;
and (*right*) a detail of a cross-shaft at Middleton; all in
Yorkshire

belong to the same tradition, but few achieve even the quality of the Newgate
stone. Indeed, *pace* Lang, it is hard to see the sculpture of northern England in
this period as anything more than a pale reflection of the mainstream styles
which appear elsewhere – in Scandinavia and in England.

Generally the Jellinge style is rare outside Yorkshire and Teesside. It hardly
occurs in Cumbria (although it might be recognized at Aspatria). In the south
of England it occurs in a modified but rather degraded form on a plate from a
house-shaped casket now in the British Museum, an object which displays
charmless animals executed with supreme incompetence by a craftsman
struggling to attain a standard of which he was clearly incapable. Jellinge
elements can be identified: the double contour of the bodies, the suspicion of a
lip-lappet on one of them, the irregular interlace and the ring encircling the
point where leg and neck cross. The Anglo-Saxon roots of this style can be seen
in the use of niello inlay, the beaded borders which divide the fields, the spaces
for dome-headed rivets and more particularly in the speckled, sub-triangular
bodies of the animals which are so clearly derived from the Trewhiddle style.

178 Disc brooch from Canterbury. Diameter 14.2 cm. (London, British Museum)

179 *Above right*: plates from a house-shaped casket. Length of base plate 12.6 cm. (London, British Museum)

Other objects decorated in a similar style include the King's School, Canterbury, disc brooch and the Sittingbourne, Kent, *seax* or dagger. (We have already seen parallels to this style in Scandinavia on the Austris Brooch.)

Rarely is such a marriage of Anglo-Saxon and Scandinavian styles so clearly displayed as in this metalwork, but occasionally, as in one fragmented cross-shaft from St Alkmund's church, Derby, the same synthesis may be seen in stone sculpture. One of the main faces of this stone displays an animal which has many of the full-bodied characteristics of the Anglo-Saxon style of the ninth century, yet it has the double contour and irregular interlace typical of the Jellinge style. A much clearer example occurs on another face of the cross-shaft, where one of the animals in a modified 'beast-chain' is more distinctly executed in the Jellinge taste, with its ribbon-like body, double contours, suspicion of a lip-lappet and irregular interlaced limbs and ribbons. It is hardly surprising to find such a stone in one of the main centres of the Danelaw (Derby was one of the towns which formed the Scandinavian polity known as the Five Boroughs), but the presence of the metalwork in the south of England is something of a puzzle – were the objects perhaps produced in what was by then Danish Mercia? Perhaps not, because there is some stone sculpture from the south of England, as for example at Steventon, Hampshire, which bears animals which have many characteristics of the Jellinge style, although their heads are of Anglo-Saxon character. This shaft stands in a relationship to the Jellinge style similar to that of the casket-plates – and there can be little doubt that it was produced in southern England. This stone is not unique in southern England in its synthesis of the two styles: even more pronounced Jellinge elements are present, for example, on one of the cross-shafts from Ramsbury, Wiltshire.

180, 1[8]

182

135

146

In many of its details the Jellinge style is closely related to the Mammen style, which takes its name from an axe found in a grave at Mammen in Denmark. The Mammen style is best seen in the Isle of Man (on crosses from Kirk Braddan for example). It is rarely encountered in English sculpture. A classic example of the style is, however, found on a bone belt-slide from the River Thames, at London. The human figure displayed here bears many of the details of the style; the pelleted body, the great shell-spiral hips and the frond-like extensions of the motif – but whether it was made in England or Denmark is not known. Occasionally the style occurs in stone sculpture – on the slab from Levisham, Yorkshire, on a stone from Workington and perhaps, dimly, on a cross-shaft from St Oswald's Priory, Gloucester. This style was developed in Scandinavia in the middle years of the tenth century and it is presumably for this reason that it is rarely encountered in England, for by the 950s relations

182 Carved stone at Steventon Manor,
Hampshire.
Height 88 cm

180, 181 Two views of a fragmentary cross-shaft from St Alkmund, Derby. Height 75 cm. (Derby, Museums and Art Gallery)

183 Detail of slab at Levisham, North Yorkshire

184 Three 'hog-back' tombstones at All Saints, Brompton, Yorkshire. Length of nearest stone 1.2 m

with Scandinavia had become more tenuous as the Scandinavian polity collapsed and as the strong influence of the Anglo-Saxon Winchester style became more apparent.

The styles discussed so far, while appearing comparatively rarely in the sculpture of the Scandinavian areas of England, are important in that they provide a chronological framework against which some of the northern English stone-carving can be placed. This is not the place to consider the methods by which the chronology of the Scandinavian styles has been erected. Suffice it to say that the Borre style flourished from the early ninth to the second half of the tenth century and the Jellinge style from c.875 to the second half of the tenth century. It should be pointed out, however, that these dates are to some extent based on the English contexts in which the styles are found and it can be difficult not to indulge in circular arguments. The Mammen style brackets a period from say 950 to 1010, a chronological position based largely on Danish evidence. The most important dating problems concern the Jellinge style. There has been much discussion concerning its earliest appearance in England, although the few finds from York have solved at least some of the riddles concerning it. There seems no reason to doubt the fact that the Jellinge

style must have made its first impact in England before the end of the ninth century and that by 900 at the latest there was a well established Jellinge style in England. It may well have been introduced through Scandinavian-controlled towns – York and Derby for example – and must soon have spread thence into the countryside.

The vast majority of motifs which appear on Anglo-Scandinavian sculpture have little to do with the three styles described above. Other less diagnostic patterns – interlace particularly – appear in careless (and rather crude) profusion on the sculpture, as do representations of human and possibly of legendary or mystic figures, some allegedly related to the Scandinavian pantheon. One particular form of monument is itself so striking that it deserves mention in its own right before we turn to the figural art. A fair number of tomb-stones in northern England are of the type known as 'hog-backs', the classic examples of which are those from Brompton, Yorkshire. They are house-shaped, with curved roof-ridge and sides, in imitation of buildings known both in England and Scandinavia. Some of them have, as terminals, muzzled bears which are among the rare representations from the Anglo-Saxon period of animals in natural form. Many are executed in a highly competent fashion, some are embellished with historiated scenes or zoomorphic ornament; some are crudely produced. These monuments may have their origin in wooden or stone shrine-tombs (like the Hedda Stone from Peterborough) or even in the stone repertoire of the Picts but, whatever their origins, the form was Anglo-Scandinavian in its inspiration.

Apart from the hog-backs, most of the other stone monuments of the North follow traditional forms – cross-shafts and recumbent slabs. The animal styles discussed above appear on them but the monuments themselves have in some cases been set in typological series based on the form of the cross-heads and even (in the case of Cumbria) on the decoration applied to these heads. Attempts to set other motifs in a chronological framework have never proved satisfactory; only a group of rather crude carvings from Durham can in all probability be dated on historical grounds to between 998 and 1083, but this is very much a local school (p. 200).

Christian and pagan tradition in the North

It is perhaps better then to examine the other ornament of northern sculpture in iconographic terms, as there are so few stylistically diagnostic details to order them in either chronological or regional terms. In considering this ornament it is best to proceed from the known to the unknown. First, there are representations of certain Christian motifs: the Crucifixion, the vine-scroll, the *agnus dei* and the Fall of Man can be clearly recognized. Other scenes (the martyrdom of St Peter, the five wounds of Christ, the sacrifice of Isaac, the death of Isaiah, and David as harpist) have been recognized with great ingenuity, but with perhaps less confidence. Second, there are scenes of pagan significance: Thor fishing, at Gosforth, Cumberland; Weland and scenes from the Sigurd cycle, at Halton, Lancashire; and Midgarðsorm (the world serpent), at Lowther, Westmorland, are the most convincing examples of these. Other suggested identifications include portrayals of Odinn, of the doom of the gods (Ragnarǫk), Gunnar in the snake pit and so on; identifications sometimes based perhaps more on imagination than on incontrovertible argument.

184

185 Detail of the Gosforth 'fishing stone'. Thor is fishing with an ox-head with which he catches the world serpent

187–9

185

186 The Gosforth Cross, Cumberland.
Height 4.4 m

Such sculptures, whether or not their iconography has been satisfactorily identified, are so crude as to be of little interest to the style historian but are of importance in understanding the blending of religions in the Scandinavian areas of England. Scandinavian pagan ideas were taken into the Christian iconography in the late ninth and early tenth century, as for example on the Gosforth Cross. On the eastern face is a Crucifixion scene with Longinus and (possibly) Mary at the foot of the cross. All the other scenes are related to the Ragnarǫk cycle which tells the mythological Norse story of the destruction of the gods (a cycle which can be interpreted in a Christian sense in terms of doomsday). On the basis of later Icelandic sources we may tentatively identify scenes from the cycle – the sun being swallowed by monsters, Heimdallr blowing his horn to wake the gods, the bound Fenris-wolf, Vidarr killing Fenris-wolf, and so on. The syncretic nature of the iconography (if correctly interpreted), with its relation between Ragnarǫk, the Crucifixion and the Last Judgement, is sophisticated and well worked out. The apparent coarseness of the images on Gosforth and elsewhere may, as Richard Bailey has pointed out, have been softened and the image made more explicit by the use of paint, traces of which are found on many stones of this period. It is a strange and fascinating art, but one which cannot be fully interpreted because of missing evidence.

186

Workshops

As a pendant to this discussion of northern sculpture of the Scandinavian period mention should be made of the intricate study and interpretation of the methods of construction and transmission of the patterns and motifs. Richard Bailey has proposed that in many cases templates were used to construct the ornament and has recognized schools of craftsmen using common templates: one such he sees as serving the Yorkshire churches of Northallerton, Brompton and Kirklevington, as well as Sockburn in Co. Durham, and has tentatively suggested other schools (one serving communities as far apart as Lancaster and Aspatria in Cumberland, separated by some eighty miles). Lang questioned Bailey's thesis in a lecture delivered to the British Association at York in 1981, in which he proposed that many patterns were constructed not from templates, but from a series of bored or punched points on which a grid could be laid out. He has identified a number of stones on which such holes appear, and proposed that such holes could be repaired before painting by the use of a gesso or cement filler. Until this paper and its complicated arguments are published the two possibilities remain open, but it is as well to remember the marking out of manuscript ornament at an earlier date, which was certainly not based on the use of templates (see p. 38).

Regional groupings and workshops can, however, be recognized with some degree of certainty. The close similarity of style between the Ryedale crosses at Middleton, Sinnington, Pickering and Ellerburn has already been mentioned. A close examination of the forms of the crosses and their shafts, and of their ornament and design, enabled Collingwood and later Bailey to pick out other regional groups: circle-headed crosses in Cumbria and another group in Cheshire, for example. But such recognition has rarely been attempted and a great deal of work remains to be done.

The sculpture and metalwork discussed so far in this chapter must largely belong to the late ninth and first half of the tenth century. But it should be remembered that there was a major Scandinavian presence in the north of

187 Reconstructed cross in St Andrew,
Auckland, Co. Durham. Height 1 m

188, 189 Two views of the fragmentary cross-shaft at
Aycliffe, Co. Durham

151

England long after the English had re-conquered it. Later Scandinavian styles are rarely found in this area (the slab at Otley, Yorkshire, is a rare exception) but it is almost certain that sculpture was still being produced in a bastard Scandinavian style well on into the eleventh century. There is little sculpture decorated in anything approaching the contemporary southern English style – the Winchester style – in the North and (apart from the interesting group of carvings from Durham discussed below) little sculpture of any innovatory interest appears in the North until after the Norman Conquest.

Alfred and his successors

The scruffy sculpture of the north of England in the years after 900 stands in sharp contrast to the glitter, sensitivity and competence of the art of the south in the same period. This has rightly been labelled 'the golden age of English art'. The innovatory elements may not be as original as those of the period of the Conversion, but the variety and brilliance of the images created during this period show an eclecticism and a manual skill which raised the flagging standards of Anglo-Saxon art. Although it drew much of its inspiration from the Continent, something survives of the lively aspects of the earlier English art – particularly in initials and plant-scrolls. The art must be seen against the general background of the history of the country after the settlement of the Danelaw and the establishment of the uneasy peace created by Alfred.

The importance of Alfred in the history of England is undoubted; that he encouraged a renaissance of learning, of law, of religion and the vernacular language is well documented. His was, however, a reign of reverses, of dynastic tensions, of foreign invasions and of political juggling. Despite all the tribulations which he encountered he managed to lay the foundations for the spectacular achievements of his successors as king. His position as a heroic king is secure; his position as a dedicated and literary ruler is unique in the second half of the first millennium. It is impossible, however, to recognize any major contribution made by the king to the art of the period. One major piece, and one alone – the Alfred Jewel – can be ascribed to his reign with some element of confidence and even possibly to his patronage, but, as we have seen, no major illuminated manuscript can be so ascribed.

Alfred's successors, Edward the Elder and Athelstan, built on his foundations. They it was who reconquered the Danish areas and consolidated a kingdom of England. Edward at the time of his death had control over most of England south of the Humber – he had not only secured the allegiance of the Danish settlers but had even (after the death of the formidable Lady Æthelflæd) reduced to nothing the pretensions of any member of the Mercian royal house to rule middle England. He had successes against the Northumbrian kings, but the Dublin–York Scandinavian axis was strongly situated by 919 and formed a very real challenge to his further political ambitions. He had, however, begun the great task of converting the kingdom of Wessex into the kingdom of England, a task which was fulfilled by his eldest son Athelstan, who was crowned at Kingston-on-Thames in 925.

Athelstan consolidated his father's *coup de main* in Mercia and, in a complicated series of campaigns, established control over Northumbria. His control was often insecure, but, after the battle of Brunanburh in 937, Athelstan was *de facto* ruler of the whole of England. Treading carefully, Athelstan took over his northern kingdom, continuing as his forebears had done to extend close relationships with the Continent, which had similar problems. He drew strength from political meddling in Frankish affairs, which culminated in a nice political alliance when his nephew Louis d'Outremer was established on the West Frankish throne in 936.

Athelstan's death in 939 was a signal for the Scandinavians to have one final attempt to wrest political control from the English. They invaded Mercia and were for a time successful; but, under the leadership of the surviving son of Edward the Elder (Eadred), Eric Bloodaxe, the last Norse king of York, was beaten and expelled in 954. Eadred thus became, as he so sonorously described himself, 'King, Emperor of the Anglo-Saxons and Northumbrians, Governor of the pagans, Defender of the Britons'.

These were the men who established the political hegemony of England. They were tough, sometimes ruthless, but not uncultivated. Athelstan's patronage of the Church, his code of laws, the elasticity of his social and political thinking, show him, for example, to be an innovator in areas quite different from those of Alfred. He is a much underestimated figure, a man of taste in things artistic, a generous and powerful ruler. Edgar, who came to the throne in 959, is portrayed as the successor to Alfred in learning and patronage. His was a glorious reign, but he was presented by his predecessors with a comparatively peaceful country, a stable legal system and a partially reformed Church. On this he built. While we must not underestimate Edgar's achievements it is as well to realize that the machine he inherited was well designed and 'ready to roll'.

Who then was Edgar, and what did he do? We must understand his reign, as it produced some of the highest achievements in painting and sculpture ever seen in England. His short reign (he died in 975) was devoid of political or military trauma, in itself no mean feat. His power was undoubted. His late coronation at Bath (on Whit Sunday, 973) and a subsequent ceremony in the same year, when he was rowed on the River Dee by six 'kings', illustrated his political stature not only in England but in the Celtic lands to the west and north. But, in Stenton's words, 'he was never required to defend English civilization against barbarians from over the sea, nor to deal with the problems raised by the existence of a barbarian state within England itself. His part in history was to maintain the peace established in England by earlier kings.' His stature as a ruler was certainly less than that of Alfred or Athelstan. His good fortune was that he was in the right place at the right time and with the right ideas to carry through a major reform of the English Church. He has thus been celebrated ever since as a great king, first by monastic historians and then by historians who believed what was written about him. In truth the reform had already started by the time he came to the throne; he was the man who carried it through with men and machinery already available.

The tenth century was a period of Church reform on the Continent; indeed the foundation of the Abbey of Cluny in 910 may perhaps be taken as a signal of the start of the reform movement. One of the monasteries influenced by Cluny was Fleury (already as has been shown in contact with England), which received a number of high-born English clergy. Oda, bishop of Ramsbury and later archbishop of Canterbury, spent some time there and sent his nephew Oswald, later bishop of Worcester and archbishop of York, to learn the Rule there. The reform party included Dunstan, abbot of Glastonbury (who for a short time was in exile at another of the Cluny-influenced houses, St Peter's,

Ghent), and Æthelwold, the *de facto* leader of the group, who re-founded the monastery of Abingdon. When Edgar became king he appointed Dunstan to Canterbury and a little later Æthelwold was moved to the see of Winchester (the major royal seat of England). With Oswald at Worcester, these three great clerical magnates ruled and reformed the Church under the patronage and with the active support of the king. The reform was intended to bring the monasteries back to the Rule of St Benedict; poverty, chastity and fasting were the three main virtues – together naturally with obedience. The monasteries were taken out of secular control, celibacy was enforced and, although family and influence still counted for much in matters of ecclesiastical preferment, a more regular, less worldly (even fanatical) Rule was introduced. Towards the end of Edgar's reign, perhaps in 973, a great council was held at Winchester as a result of which a document of reform, the *Regularis Concordia*, was produced, attempting in some measure to lay down Rules for the great monastic houses of England, to codify the revival initiated by Dunstan when he became abbot of Glastonbury some thirty years before. All this was done with informed and strong royal support.

There is a considerable discussion about the side effects of this reform, but in its central principles it succeeded; by the end of the century most of the bishops were monks who had been trained in the reformed monasteries, and most of the great monasteries of England (those which were to survive until the English Reformation) had been founded. Whether learning was greatly improved as a result of the reform is open to question; it has been called 'an age of intellectual breadth and clarity', but some critics are less flattering, castigating its leaders for scholarly and Biblical ignorance and incompetence in Latin. It was perhaps as a result of the reform that the English language flowered in the late tenth and early eleventh century and it may be that scholarship and Latinity flourished more fully in the period after Edgar. It is quite clear, however, that during Edgar's reign one of the greatest pieces of English art was produced – the Benedictional of St Æthelwold. The tenth century produced great English art, but for this not all the praise should go to Edgar and his bishops. Its foundations were laid early in the century – perhaps even earlier, in the reign of Alfred – and, although the story of the pre-Edgar period can only be tenuously drawn together, it was the patrons of the early part of the tenth century who provided the impetus which produced the great glories of what is known as the Winchester school.

The Winchester style – the first phase

The origins of the Winchester style are best seen in the magnificent embroideries found in the coffin of St Cuthbert (see above, p. 49ff.). The embroideries consist of a stole, a maniple and a girdle (sometimes known as the small maniple; it is probably only the ornamental pendant of a girdle). The embroideries are worked in coloured silks and gold thread, the backing or ground being a whitish silk. The colours of the silks are dark green, dark brown, blue, brownish-red and red, all used with gold thread twisted on a core of red silk. These three pieces were almost certainly those given by Athelstan in c.934 to the Community of St Cuthbert in its new home at Chester-le-Street. The rich gifts listed in the *Historia de Sancto Cuthberto* include *unam stolam cum manipulo* (a stole and maniple) and a *cingulum* (girdle). Inscriptions on the stole and maniple record that they were made by the command of Queen

Ælfflaed for Frithestan, bishop of Winchester. Ælfflaed, Athelstan's step-mother, died before 916 and Frithestan became bishop in 909. In all probability, therefore, the embroideries were made between 909 and 916. The embroideries (now in the Treasury of Durham Cathedral) are of breathtaking brilliance and quality; in the words of Mrs Plenderleith they are 'in the front rank of embroidery of any period'.

The maniple is almost complete; 82 cm long exclusive of the fringe. In the centre of the strip is a quatrefoil containing the hand of God and flanked by two full-length figures: St Gregory and his attendant deacon, Peter, and St Sixtus and his deacon, Laurence. Square panels at the ends portray half-length figures of St John the Baptist and St John the Evangelist. Each figure is identified by inscription. The stole is not complete: seven fragments only remain. In the centre of the stole is a quatrefoil containing the hands of God, which is flanked by full-length figures of the major and minor prophets – originally sixteen in all. The half-length figures in the terminal panels are St James and St Thomas and on the reverse of these two panels (as on the maniple) are the inscriptions to Ælfflaed and Frithestan. The girdle, which is only 63 cm long, consists of two strips of embroidery with slightly expanded ends stitched together. This is decorated with a tree-like pattern with acanthus leaves and small bird-like figures.

All three strips of silk embroidery were plainly executed by the same hand. The iconography is clear, but complicated. The prophets represented are only seen in such company on the coronation mantle of the kings of Hungary, which apparently dates from the early eleventh century. This at least suggests that there was at this time an iconography clearly distinct from that seen in the manuscripts.

The style of the embroideries is highly individual. The figures are slender and their height is accentuated by the skilful use of the lines which depict the fold of the drapery. The figures stand on formalized rocky ground and are separated by a flourish of acanthus. The inscriptions read across the body, the letters being distributed in the available space. The stance and elongated nature of the figures are diagnostic of this style and seem to have no immediate forerunners. There is certainly no strain in Anglo-Saxon art of the ninth century which relates to this style, nor is there any obvious Carolingian prototype. Unconvincing attempts have been made to derive the style from Sassanian and Byzantine sources, but it seems to have been developed for ecclesiastical robes either in England or on the Continent and has little relationship to anything that has come before. One interesting parallel is a fragment of wall-painting found on a stone re-used in the building of the New Minster at Winchester (dating therefore earlier than c.903).

The painting is executed in red, yellow, white and black directly on the surface of the stone (there is no trace of a gesso base). At one side a raised border survives which forms part of the frame to the main field. This has a geometric repeat pattern of white semi-circles on a black background – a form of ornament familiar in Carolingian manuscripts. Despite these parallels the figures in the main field (of which only one head and the remains of the shoulders of two others survive) seem closer to the Cuthbert embroideries, particularly in the treatment of eyes, nose and hair. This parallel cannot be pushed too far as the wall-painting presents a group scene – possibly a choir of angels – of a type paralleled in earlier Carolingian manuscripts. Nevertheless,

190 The prophet Daniel, from St Cuthbert's stole (Durham, Cathedral Treasury)

155

it is clear that the Winchester painting may be a missing link between the early ninth century and the St Cuthbert textiles.

One of the more important elements of the decoration of the St Cuthbert textiles is the emergence for the first time of acanthus ornament in a Winchester context. This lush leaf decoration was to dominate the art of the tenth century in southern England. It is arguably first encountered in an English context on the back of the Alfred Jewel and is found in one or two other metalwork contexts, demonstrating that it was already reasonably well-known in ninth-century England. The motif was derived directly from Carolingian sources, although the exuberance that is achieved in the Winchester environment was never matched on the Continent.

The next most important monument of early tenth-century English art is a copy of Bede's *Life of St Cuthbert* (Cambridge, Corpus Christi College, 183). This manuscript (which measures 29 × 19 cm) has a framed full-page frontispiece which almost certainly represents Athelstan presenting the book to St Cuthbert. It is normally identified with the manuscript mentioned in the *Historia de Sancto Cuthberto* as donated by the king when he visited St Cuthbert's shrine at Chester-le-Street *c*.934 (see above, p. 154). Palaeographically it is possible to say that the book was produced in southern England, probably at Winchester. The manuscript contains numerous small ornamented initials and some rather larger ones. The colours used are rust brown, pale purple, yellow, light blue and orange. The frontispiece is the earliest surviving presentation portrait in English art. To the left, the bowed figure of a king presents the book to a nimbed saint, the composition being placed against an architectural background of a type found in continental sources. The figure of the saint (presumably Cuthbert) has been likened to the figures on the stole and maniple of St Cuthbert and this comparison seems valid, although the position of the feet is different. The scrolls of the frame vary greatly; they include plain scrolls with acanthus leaves, an acanthus plant-scroll, inhabited and partially inhabited scrolls and a tree-scroll with birds. The English origins of the plant-scrolls are obvious (particularly the origins of the inhabited scrolls), the only flavour of the Continent being the acanthus leaves – a motif, however, well-known in England for more than a generation. The plant-scrolls are tightly contained within borders and no attempt is made by the artist to allow them to escape from the frame, as happens only thirty or so years later in great Winchester style manuscripts like the Benedictional of St Æthelwold.

191 The back of the Alfred Jewel. See pls. 121, 122. Length 8 cm. (Oxford, Ashmolean Museum)

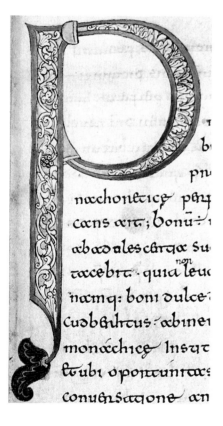

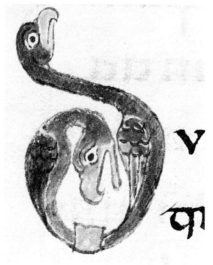

192, 193 Ornamented initials from Bede's *Life of St Cuthbert* (Cambridge, Corpus Christi College, 183, ff. 6r and 42v)

191

203

192, 1

194 Ornamented initial from the Barberini Gospels
(Rome, Biblioteca Vaticana, Barb. Lat. 570, fol. 7r)

195, 196 Ornamented initials from a
manuscript of Bede's *Ecclesiastical
history*
(Oxford, Bodleian Library, Tanner 10,
ff. 43r and 54r)

The composition of the dedication page is clumsy and stiff. It is poorly laid out and has an unexciting range of colours. But it does herald a breakthrough in manuscript art. It may be an accident of survival that we have no really great religious manuscripts of the period between the Canterbury Bible and the second quarter of the tenth century – about a hundred years; whether there were any we shall probably never know. Here, however, we see the first glimpse of one of the great schools of English art and, what is more, we glimpse the origins of that school. First, we see the Carolingian influence, represented in the acanthus leaves and, probably, in the composition of the page. But, second, the native taste is seen not only in the inhabited scroll, but also in the initials. It is true that some of the initials (pl. 192, for example) are strictly Carolingian in inspiration, but others hark back to the letters which embellish the Barberini Gospels and have terminal animal heads, biting tendrils and other English elements. These initials and those in other manuscripts – Bodleian Library Tanner 10 particularly – in some cases develop into something close to a traditional vine-scroll. The use of human figures in the formation of some of the letters is a strange phenomenon certainly not encountered on the Continent and (although we might see here a distant echo of Byzantium) the whole structure and apparent indiscipline of design points back to the early ninth century, and particularly to the Barberini Gospels. Gradually more continental elements are introduced as acanthus ornament appears, for example, in what is probably a Winchester manuscript, Bodleian Library Junius 27. But even here the inhabited vine-scroll and historiated initials (first noted in the Leningrad Bede) can be traced back to earlier English art.

194

195, 196

212–15

197 *Seax* (a form of dagger), from Sittingbourne, Kent. Length 32.3 cm. (London, British Museum)

Metalwork and ivory

This continuity and overlap can perhaps best be seen in the metalwork. The Alfred Jewel, although decorated on the back with an acanthus motif, has an animal-headed socket very similar to a series of such heads on ninth-century strap-ends and on such objects as the Strickland Brooch. Another overlap occurs on a knife-like dagger (of the type known as a *seax*) from Sittingbourne, Kent. This object is inlaid with different metals to produce the polychrome effect mentioned in the discussion of the Strickland Brooch. The silver plates are inlaid with animal and leaf ornament derived from the Trewhiddle tradition, but one panel bears a fully developed Carolingian acanthus-leaf pattern, florid and fleshy. (This *seax*, incidentally, has an inscription on one side which names the maker, Biorhthelm, while the side illustrated names the owner, Sigebereht.)

Silver plates are also inlaid in panels at the base of a bronze censer-cover from Canterbury. Here again florid acanthus ornament is found, and (like the Sittingbourne panel) these are also inlaid with niello. The censer-cover is interesting in more ways than one. Its form, which is paralleled on the Pershore censer-cover and elsewhere, is architectural; it takes the shape of a church tower of a rare form capped by what is known as a 'Rhenish helm'. Such a cap survives on the tower at Sompting, Sussex (which, being partly built of Caen stone, must date from just after the Norman Conquest) and may also have been used on the tower of St Bene't's, Cambridge. The form is quite simple; on each face is a gable, from the apex of which rise the ridges of a pyramidal roof; the roof is carried down into the spaces between the gables to form lozenge-shaped fields. The object is cast in openwork and the fields are filled with

122

197

208

209

279

198 Pen-case of walrus ivory. Length 23.5 cm. (London, British Museum)

199, 200 *Right*: detail of the binding of the Henry II Gospels (Munich, Bayerisches Staatsbibliothek, Cod. Lat. 4454). *Far right*: Strap end from Winchester. Length 4 cm

201, 202 Purse-shaped reliquary from Winchester, with a drawing of the reconstructed opposite face. Height 17.5 cm (Winchester City Museum)

125

195, 196

210

199

211

200

198

contorted birds and animals, which to some extent are paralleled on the Wolverhampton Pillar and are not dissimilar, for example, to the birds and animals portrayed in Bodleian Library Tanner 10. There is also a correspondence with the tree-scroll pattern in the Corpus Christi Bede. This rather chunky style is seen in a number of pieces of metalwork, on a censer-cover of the same form from London; on a small gilt-bronze spouted jug; on gold plates in the cover of the Henry II Gospels in Munich; on a couple of sword hilts from Sweden and on a series of strap ends (in both metal and ivory), including a splendid example from Winchester, which has a slightly attenuated acanthus ornament together with pecking birds and backward-looking quadrupeds. This seems to be a style of south-east England in the first half of the tenth century.

A delicate walrus ivory pen-case from London, usually dated to the eleventh century, may also belong to this group. On the lid is an elegant acanthus scroll with contorted birds and animals set symmetrically on either side of a stem; at one end is a large animal mask producing a forked tongue which covers two animals that in many ways resemble ninth- or tenth-century Scandinavian 'gripping beasts'. If this resemblance is not coincidental it could support a claim for the lid to be of tenth-century date, a claim which might be strengthened by parallels with the probably rather earlier ornament of the Corpus Christi Bede. The historiated ornament of the side panels of the case is difficult to parallel, but in detail could be placed in the tenth century. We must be careful, however, of committing too much weight to the lack of parallels for such ornament in the eleventh century, but the presence of good parallels for the zoomorphic and acanthus ornament at least argues for the possibility of a tenth-century date.

201, 202

A remarkable piece of metalwork excavated in an early tenth-century context is the Winchester purse-shaped reliquary, decorated with ornamented gilt-copper sheets. Embossed on the surface of one face is acanthus ornament made up from three pieces cut from a single strip of metal. The ends of the object are plain but a seated figure of Christ can be reconstructed on the much damaged front. The acanthus ornament is very close in style to that encountered in Carolingian contexts on the Continent, but it is quite possible that it is an English copy of the motif and that the reliquary was made – perhaps in Winchester – in the late ninth or early tenth century.

The Benedictional of St Æthelwold
and Winchester painting

The sophisticated acanthus ornament of this reliquary may serve to introduce the florid and colourful acanthus ornament of the high Winchester style, seen at its apogee in the art of the Benedictional of St Æthelwold (British Library, Add.49598). The origin of the manuscript is described in a long and adulatory introductory poem written in golden capitals, of which the following is important from our point of view:

> A bishop, the great Æthelwold, whom the Lord had made patron of Winchester, ordered a certain monk subject to him to write the present book . . . Let all who look upon this book pray always that . . . I may abide in heaven – Godeman the scribe, as a suppliant asks this.

The Benedictional was the book of episcopal blessings of Bishop Æthelwold,

203 *Opposite*: King Athelstan presenting Bede's *Life of St Cuthbert* to the saint (Cambridge, Corpus Christi College, 183, fol. 1v). 29 × 19 cm. See p. 156

204 Fragment of wall-painting from a stone re-used in the foundations of the New Minster, Winchester. Length 58.6 cm (Winchester City Museum). See p. 155

205–7 Three details from the stole and maniple found in the tomb of St Cuthbert, Durham Cathedral: Peter the Deacon, the Prophet Amos and (*opposite*), much enlarged, St John the Evangelist (Durham Cathedral). See pp. 154–5

208, 209 Two bronze censer-covers in the shape of towers.
Left: from Canterbury, height 11.5 cm; *right*: from Pershore, Worcestershire, height 9.7 cm. They both imitate the 'Rhenish helm' type of roof (see pl. 279) (Both London, British Museum).
See p. 158

210 Gilt bronze jug from London. Height 9.5 cm (London, British Museum). See p. 160

211 Sword hilt, from Dybäck, Ö Vemmenhög, Skåne, Sweden (Stockholm, Statens Historiska Museum). See p. 160

212–15 Ornamented initials from a Psalter, probably
painted at Winchester.
Oxford, Bodleian Library, Junius 27, ff. 135v (*left, top
and bottom*), 118r (*right, top*), 148v (*right, bottom*).
See p. 157

216 Figure of St Ætheldreda, from the Benedictional of
St Æthelwold
(London, British Library, Add. 49598, fol. 90v).
29 × 22.5 cm. See pp. 160, 169

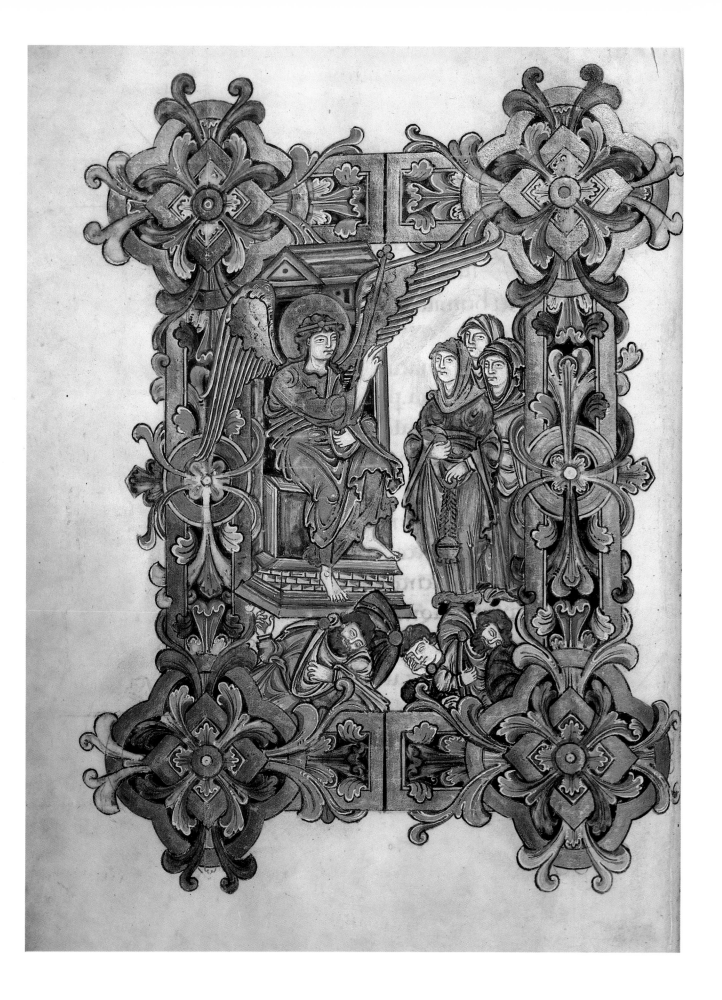

who as we have seen was bishop of Winchester and one of the main reformers of the English Church in the reign of Edgar. The book, therefore, must be dated to the period of his episcopacy (963–85), and Francis Wormald pointed out that a reference to miracles recently performed at the shrine of St Swithun would suggest that the book was put together after 971 when the saint was translated. It is one of the most remarkable of all English manuscripts; crisp and clean, it is comparatively small, measuring 29 × 22.5 cm, and is of a luxury which makes one question the particular ideal of the Benedictine Rule so prized by Æthelwold. It has twenty-eight pages of full illumination, each set within an ornamental frame, as well as an ornamental text. It also has nineteen pages within decorative frames, one historiated initial of Christ in Majesty and one historiated initial (Christ blessing) within a frame. Originally there were probably another fifteen fully illuminated pages and two more bordered pages. All are sumptuously coloured in rich tones which range from pink to mauve, from deep indigo to light green, brown, yellow and red; the colours are often overpainted to add perspective and gold and silver are used liberally. The manuscript itself is written in Carolingian minuscule, which was at this time introduced into the country, and which illustrates the French roots of the reform movement. The miniatures celebrate various feasts, portraying the saint or person honoured. Iconographically they are closely related to late Carolingian ivories of the school of Metz, but other influences are drawn from the eastern Early Christian world and there is a startling amount of English invention in the make-up of the art of the book. Little on the Continent prepares us for the decorative whole, which is the result of Anglo-Saxon innovatory ambition. The figural drawing has a slightly ethereal quality, the clothes dominate the person and the careful shading and linear quality imparted to the dress sometimes detract from portraiture, the faces often tending towards pure decoration, although they are lightly and sensitively delineated in fresh colours. The frames of the page are heavy and occasionally ebullient, bursting in a disciplined if luxurious fashion beyond the strict confines of the outline in a mass of acanthus leaves (particularly seen round the representation of St Etheldreda). The last full-page illumination in the book, which depicts a bishop blessing a church, is a strange combination of full colour and line drawing, the importance of the chief figure being emphasized by the use of rich colour. The line drawing is related to another Anglo-Saxon tradition examined below (p. 179ff.).

Two manuscripts are so closely related to the Benedictional of St Æthelwold that they must have been produced within a few years of it. They are the Benedictional and Pontifical of Archbishop Robert of Jumièges (Rouen, Bibliothèque municipale, Y.7(369)) and another Benedictional, identical in text but simpler in decoration to the Benedictional of St Æthelwold (Paris, Bibliothèque Nationale, lat.987). Only three Winchester miniatures survive in the Benedictional of Archbishop Robert; they are close copies of similar scenes in Æthelwold's book, save that their iconography is rather simpler. The figural drawing is perhaps less light-handed than that of the other manuscript, but the colour range is similar and the heavy foliate frames are almost identical in spirit. It is clear from liturgical evidence that the manuscript was written in Winchester, possibly at the order of Æthelwold himself; the association with Archbishop Robert (and even the identification of Robert) has sometimes been challenged.

217 *Opposite*: the three Marys at the tomb, from the Benedictional and Pontifical of Robert of Jumièges (Rouen, Bibliothèque municipale, Y. 7 (369), fol. 21v)

218

219

217

218 *Overleaf*: St Peter with two Apostles, from the Benedictional of St Æthelwold (London, British Library, Add. 49598, fol. 4r). 29 × 22.5 cm

219 A bishop pronouncing a blessing, from the Benedictional of St Æthelwold (London, British Library, Add. 49598, fol. 118v). 29 × 22.5 cm

repleri · ut cum eis caelestis spon
si thalamum ualeatis ingre
di · quod ipse ·

171

These books are the key to the florid Winchester style and stand at the head of a long line of English manuscripts which extend in the same tradition into the twelfth century. The style was adopted by many of the reformed monastic houses – Christ Church, Canterbury; St Augustine's, Canterbury; Bury St Edmunds and Peterborough, as well as others – and, although the style seems to have had its origins as a court school in the capital of Winchester, it is encountered throughout the south of England. The influences of the Corpus Christi Bede and the Athelstan Psalter (British Library, Cotton Galba A.xviii) are evident, while the direct relationship to Carolingian art seen in these two earlier manuscripts is heightened in the Winchester group. The rather rigorous style of the court school is, however, softened by the more relaxed line of the figure drawing and the even more painterly way of adding colour, a technique perhaps derived from the Eastern Empire.

220

172

BE
A
TVS
VIR QVI NON
ABIIT IN CON
SILIOIMPIORVM

Next in development from the Benedictional of St Æthelwold is the Charter of the New Minster at Winchester (British Library, Cotton Vespasian A.viii). The New Minster was founded in 966 but stylistically and typologically the frontispiece to the charter is almost certainly later than this date, later probably than the Benedictional. The text of the manuscript is written in gold, save that the crosses in front of the list of witnesses are sometimes filled with silver. The script is neat and gives a rich impression. The display pages are coloured. The frontispiece (which is the major illumination of the manuscript) portrays Edgar, between the Virgin and St Peter, offering the charter to Christ enthroned in a golden mandorla supported by four angels. The frame consists of two bordering lines caught up in straggly acanthus of a form much more developed than that of the Benedictional. The whole border – indeed the whole picture – gives an impression of an openwork design. The palette ranges from a very light blue to purple, through red, green and brown; the shading is emphasized by contrasting coloured lines. The almost twisted posture of the king is reminiscent of the court school of Charles the Bald and is certainly much more advanced in liveliness than the rather puddingy stance of the royal donor in the Corpus Christi Bede. The charter is usually dated to 966, but it is unique in form – it is a book and not the normal single or double sheet of vellum – and was surely copied for a special, possibly ritual, function towards the end of the century. Could it for example have been placed on the altar of the New Minster as a memorial to either Æthelwold or Edgar? The fluttering nature of the acanthus ornament, which is a far cry from the compact leaves of the other Winchester manuscripts of the period of Æthelwold and earlier, is nearer to the more exuberant acanthus ornament of such manuscripts as the Sacramentary of Robert of Jumièges (Rouen, Bibliothèque municipale, Y.6(274)), which is dated after 1015 (although the manuscript has been attributed to Christ Church, Canterbury); the style itself reaches its rather stolid apotheosis in the Judith of Flanders Gospels (New York, Pierpont Morgan Library, M.709), which dates from the third quarter of the eleventh century.

The great lush service and altar books continued to be produced until after the Norman Conquest. Winchester and Canterbury were the main centres of production, but Peterborough (the Copenhagen Gospels), Winchcombe (Cambridge, University Library, Ff.I.23), Abingdon (the Warsaw Gospels and Lectionary), and Crowland (the Douce Psalter) also produced grand manuscripts. Books from other *scriptoria* are missing from our lists. Hereford, for example, once had two manuscripts attributed to it, but they are now said to have been painted in Canterbury; Glastonbury, one of the main centres of the Reform movement, certainly produced decorated manuscripts at this period, but nothing as lush as these survives; Worcester has left a hint of its scribes' ability in a single initial in a *Life of St Gregory* (British Library, Royal 6.A.VII), but Ely, York, London, Dorchester, Bury St Edmunds and a dozen other centres have left no trace of the effect of the great tenth-century 'renaissance' of English art.

No survey of English art would be complete without mention of two of the most splendid manuscripts of this richly ornamented tradition, both written at the monastery of Christ Church, Canterbury, one by a scribe who has been identified as Eadvius Basan, the other either by that scribe or by a pupil. The first is the Grimbald Gospels (British Library, Add. 34890), named after the

222 *Opposite*: Christ Triumphant, from the Douce Psalter (Oxford, Bodleian Library, Douce 296, fol. 40r)

alleged founder of the New Minster community at Winchester. The
manuscript measures 32 × 24.5 cm. It is sumptuous: reds, gold, silver, blue-
green, brown and flesh colour illuminate the great introductory pages of each
Gospel (those for St Mark's are now missing). The frames of the pages are
embellished with panels containing half-length human figures and the corners
of the pages and the centres of each side of the frame are set with roundels
containing seated figures, scenes from the Bible, angels, scenes of adoration
and so on. There is little acanthus here, the wings of most delicately drawn
angels replacing its wilder excesses. The angels themselves are lightly drawn,
with great sensitivity, their small heads and long fingers providing a delicate
balance to their elegantly contorted bodies. After the Canterbury Bible this is
the most sumptuous surviving manuscript of southern England. In many ways
the decoration harks back to the earlier manuscripts – the use of silver for
example is a marked technical parallel – and, although it was produced at
Christ Church and not at St Augustine's, there was clearly some knowledge of
the earlier tradition in the same city.

The second such manuscript is the Bury Gospels (British Library, Harley
76), a smaller, perhaps less refined, work (it measures 26.5 × 20 cm), possibly
painted for the newly founded monastery of Bury St Edmunds between 1020
and 1030. This was a royal foundation and became extremely rich. The Gospel
Book is worthy of the monastery's founders, Knut and his queen. It is
sometimes thought that the manuscript was written at Bury but it has recently
been ascribed to the school of Eadvius Basan on palaeographical grounds.
Originally it must have been one of the richest and most elaborate eleventh-
century manuscripts. It contained miniatures of the Evangelists and a full-page
decorated initial for each Gospel (all now missing save the initial letter of St
Mark) and fourteen pages of canon tables. While it has a similar colour range
to the Grimbald Gospels (save only that there is no silver in the manuscript), it
has not the same liveliness, the same freedom, as its companion piece. The
figures are heavier, the leaf ornament over-formalized and the faces of the
angels in the canon tables heavy and less refined. It has rightly been described
as looking back to the Anglo-Saxon 'renaissance' and forward to the
Romanesque. It seems to have fallen between the two.

The Bury Gospels is one of a group of manuscripts (a psalter – Arundel 155 –
in the British Library, the Eadui Codex, the Sherborne Pontifical, for example)
which, with the Grimbald Gospels, serve to show the quality of the
scriptorium of Christ Church, Canterbury. The rich, plushy manuscripts of
this group reflect the self-satisfied churchmanship of late tenth- and eleventh-
century England.

The liveliness glimpsed in the Charter of the New Minster and in the
Grimbald Gospels turns our attention back to the tenth century and the
emergence of a remarkable phenomenon, perhaps *the* most remarkable
phenomenon of English art – linear drawing – which achieved heights of
feeling and even joyousness that is totally missing from the rich, elegant
manuscripts of royal or episcopal patronage. Such manuscript drawings must
not perhaps be over-praised, but they are modest in taste and more acceptable
to modern eyes.

264

263

223

223 *Opposite*: St Benedict being
presented with his Rule by monks,
from a psalter (London, British
Library, Arundel 155, fol. 133r).
29 × 20.5 cm

Wo. Alley D.D.

tunga petra est

Uide
Altitu
dicē me
timonē
dñi do
ceboŭos

tunga penant tui.

Dunstanum memet cle
mens rogo xpe tuere
Tenarias me non sinas
sorbsisse procellas.

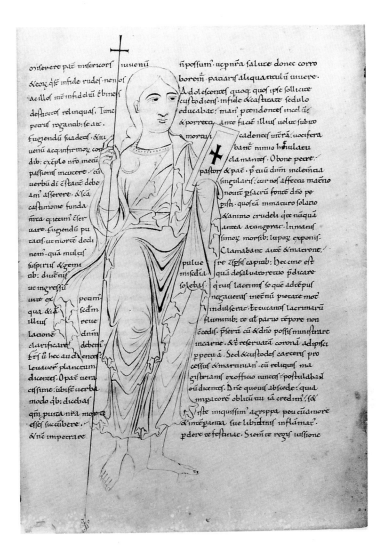

224 St Dunstan at the feet of Christ
(Oxford, Bodleian Library,
Auct.F.4.32). 24.5 × 18 cm

225 Christ
(Oxford, St John's College, 28, fol. 2r).
33 × 24 cm

Line drawing

One of the innovatory features of manuscript art in the tenth and eleventh
centuries was the lively and naturalistic depiction of the human figure, a trait
not encountered in earlier miniatures. Although there is a formalism of stance
and expression in the rich pages described above there are occasional flashes of
naturalism, as in the figural drawing of the Charter of the New Minster. The
figures drawn in simple outline are often livelier and more impromptu. The
formalism is, however, still there: take, for example, the earliest datable
drawing, St Dunstan at the feet of Christ, on a single leaf originally left blank in 224
a ninth-century manuscript now in the Bodleian Library, Oxford (Auct.
F.4.32). The page measures 24.5 × 18 cm and displays an outline drawing of
Christ with a rod and book adored by a kneeling St Dunstan. An inscription
above the figure of the kneeling monk is almost certainly in Dunstan's own
hand and the page, which was certainly at Glastonbury, was therefore
probably decorated before Dunstan went into exile in 956. A touch of red has
been added to the halo but otherwise the drawing is executed in firm brown
lines. The drawing has been described as 'monumental', but the figure of St
Dunstan relieves it of some of its ponderous quality. The style is immediately
derived from the Court school of Charlemagne, but Late Antique and
Byzantine overtones are also present.

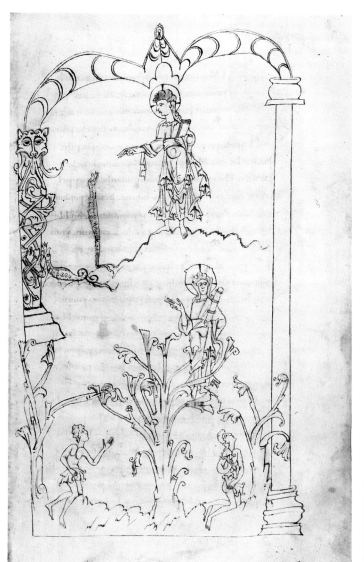

This same style is seen in a number of other books. A contemporary drawing of the Second Person of the Trinity, for example, on the flyleaf of a manuscript in Oxford (St John's College, 28) might also have been drawn at Glastonbury (although it has by some been associated with Canterbury). The style is basically that of the Winchester school; a cheaper version perhaps, but a true representative of the classic style. The style continues into the eleventh century in such manuscripts as the *Psychomachia* of Prudentius in Corpus Christi College, Cambridge (MS. 23) and more startlingly in the almost over-illustrated vernacular version of the early books of the Bible by Caedmon in the Bodleian Library, Oxford (Junius II), which was produced at Canterbury. This is a most remarkable, completely fascinating and ugly book. 'It is', to quote Barbara Raw, 'the only one of the four principal manuscripts of Old English poetry to be illustrated.' It is decorated by two hands, space being reserved at the end of the manuscript for further drawings, which were never completed. The scribe of the first hand produced thirty-eight drawings in colour outline, ranging from scenes in the Garden of Eden to Noah's Ark. The lines are firmly and confidently drawn, but in a way the style almost

225

226, 227

226, 227 Two pages from Caedmon's verse paraphrase of Genesis, drawn by the so-called 'first hand': the Garden of Eden and Noah's Ark (Oxford, Bodleian Library, Junius 11, pp. 41, 68). 32.3 × 19.5 cm

228 The story of the calling of Abraham, from Caedmon's paraphrase of Genesis, drawn by the so-called 'second hand' (Oxford, Bodleian Library, Junius 11, p. 84)

caricatures the Winchester school, the figures are heavy and drawn with abandon, the fluttering edges of the dress are almost uncontrolled and the acanthus ornament is even wilder than that in the New Minster Charter. It is a remarkable document but nobody could label it beautiful. In tradition it is more clearly related to Early Christian iconographic themes than any other contemporary manuscript, but textually it might be related to the Old English Genesis.

The second hand is much less wooden, more composed. It is clearly related 228 to another tradition which runs through English manuscripts of the late tenth and eleventh centuries and is derived from the art of the Utrecht Psalter. This manuscript (Utrecht, University Library, Script. eccl.484) belongs to the Reims 229 school and was produced by a number of hands either in Reims or in the nearby monastery of Hautvillers, probably between 816 and 823. It has been described by Dodwell as 'the most significant work of art of the whole Carolingian period'. The drawings in bistre are full of life and show a movement not achieved before in Western art; the bodies move vigorously, the trees are windblown, clouds rush restlessly across the sky, the lines are

ETCIRCUMDABOALTA
RETUUMDNE
UTAUDIAUOCEMLAU
DIS ETENARREMUNI
UERSAMIRABILIATUA
ONEDILEXIDECOREMDO
MUSTUAE ETLOCUMHA
BITATIONISGLORIAE
TUAE

NEPERDASCUMIMPIIS
ANIMAMMEAM ETCU
UIRISSANGUINUM
UITAMMEAM
INQUORUMMANIBUS
INIQUITATESSUNT
DEXTERAEORUMREPLE
TAESTMUNERIBUS

EGOAUTEININNOCEN
TIAMEAINGRESSUSSUM
REDIMEMEETMISERERE
MEI
PESMEUSSTETITINDIREC
TO INECCLESIISBENE
DICAMTEDNE

XXVI DAUID
DNSINLUMINATIO
MEAETSALUSMEA
QUEMTIMEBO
DNSPROTECTORUITAE
MEAE AQUOTREPIDABO
DUMADPROPIANTSUPER
MEINOCENTES UTEDANT
CARNESMEAS
QUITRIBULANTMEINI
MICIMEI IPSIINFIRMA

PRIUSQUAMLINE
TISUNTETCECIDERUNT
SICONSISTANTADUER
SUMMECASTRA NON
TIMEBITCORMEUM
SIEXSURGATADUERSU
MEPROELIUM INHOC
EGOSPERABO
UNAMPETIIADNOHANC
REQUIRAM UTINHA
BITEMINDOMODNI

RETUR
OMNIBUSDIEBUSUI
TAEMEAE
UTUIDEAMUOLUNTATE
DNI ETUISITEMTEMPLU
EIUS
QNMABSCONDITMEIN
TABERNACULOSUOIN
DIEMALORUM PRO
TEXITMEINABSCONDITO
TABERNACULISUI

229 Page from the Utrecht Psalter, illustrating Psalm 27: 'Though an host should encamp against me, my heart shall not fear . . . for in the time of trouble the Lord shall hide me in his pavilion'. (Utrecht, University Library, Script. eccl. 484, fol. 15r)

230

carefully graded to give depth to the subject and illusion to the composition. The figures are drawn, often in short, quick lines, with hunched backs and small heads; they hold weapons and ride on horses which are depicted most economically. The manuscript takes its inspiration from Late Antique sources through a Byzantine medium; the text has been turned into Latin, but none of the Carolingian heaviness of hand is evident in the manuscript. The Utrecht Psalter came to England at some time in the tenth century and is of interest in that a number of copies were made of it in English *scriptoria*. One copy in the British Library (Harley 603) is of relevance here. The first part of it was produced at Christ Church, Canterbury, in about 1000 by a number of artists

182

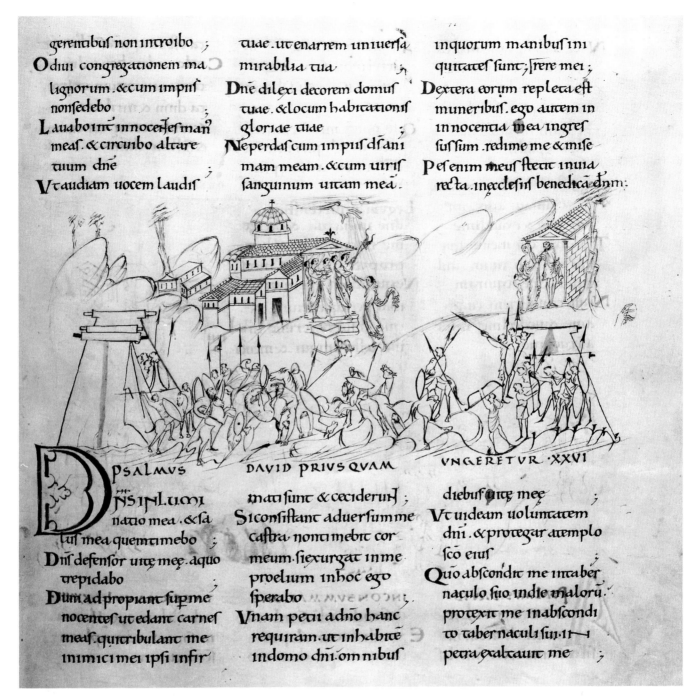

gerentibuf non introibo ;
Odiui congregationem ma
lignorum . &cum impiif
nonfedebo ;
Lauabo inï innocentïef man?
meaf . & circuibo altare
tuum dñe
Vt audiam uocem laudif

tuae . ut enarrem uniuerfa
mirabilia tua ;
Dñe dilexi decorem domuf
tuae . &locum habitacionif
gloriae tuae ;
Ne perdaf cum impiif dsani
mam meam . &cum uirif
fanguinum uitam mea .

inquorum manibuf ini
quitatef funt ; fere mei ;
Dextera eorum repleta eft
muneribuf . ego autem in
innocentia mea ingref
fuf fum . redime me & mife
Pef enim meuf ftetit inuia
recta . inecclefiif benedica dñm :

B PSALMVS
DNsinlumi
natio mea . &fa
luf mea quem timebo ;
Dñf defenfor uitæ meæ . aquo
trepidabo ;
Dum adpropiant fupme
nocentef ut edant carnef
meaf . quitribulant me
inimici mei ipfi infir

DAVID PRIVSQVAM
mati funt & ceciderunt ;
Si confiftant aduerfum me
caftra . non timebit cor
meum . fiexurgat inme
proelium inhoc ego
fperabo ;
Vnam petii adño hanc
requiram . ut inhabitë
indomo dñi . omnibuf

VNGERETVR · XXVI
diebuf uitæ meæ ;
Vt uideam uoluntatem
dñi . & protegar atemplo
fco eiuf ;
Quia abfcondit me intaber
naculo fuo indie maloru .
protexit me inabfcondi
to tabernaculi fui . it
petra exaltauit me ;

(further drawings were added in the second quarter of the eleventh century, in the last quarter of the century and in the early twelfth century). The English artist copied almost exactly the scenes portrayed in the Utrecht Psalter, although in a different coloured ink; the same liveliness is evident, but in much more frenetic, breathless form. The gestures are wild and the draperies wilder. The style of the group of manuscripts influenced by the Utrecht Psalter was the second mainstream in late Anglo-Saxon drawing, bringing a calligraphical ability to the expression of human form in landscape not previously seen in English art.

230 The same scene, copied from the Utrecht Psalter by an English scribe. (London, British Library, Harley 603, fol. 15r)

183

231 King Knut and his wife, Ælfgyfu,
presenting an altar cross: frontispiece
to the *Liber Vitae* of the New Minster,
Winchester
(London, British Library, Stowe 944,
fol. 6r). 25.5 × 14.3 cm

232 Last Judgement, from the *Liber
Vitae* of the New Minster, Winchester
(London, British Library, Stowe 944,
ff. 6v, 7r). Each page 25.5 × 14.3 cm

The Utrecht Psalter was probably not the unique model for what followed,
nor probably was Harley 603 the first manuscript to be produced in this new
impressionistic style. But the Utrecht manuscript and the style which it
represents were obviously of some importance in Canterbury. Two
Winchester manuscripts display the style brilliantly. One is a small
miscellaneous book of offices and prayers made for a deacon called Ælfwine
before 1032 (British Library, Cotton Titus D.xxvi and xxvii) and the other,
much more important, is the *Liber Vitae*, or book of donations, of the New
Minster (British Library, Stowe 944), written after 1020 by Ælsinus, a scribe of
the New Minster in the first half of the eleventh century. The frontispiece of
this manuscript in many ways reflects that of the Charter of the New Minster

and portrays Knut and his wife, Ælfgyfu, presenting an altar cross to the abbey. Flying angels hold the king's crown and queen's head-dress, and above them is a seated Christ in a mandorla flanked by St Peter and the Virgin. The next opening of the book shows an immense Last Judgement with the devil and St Peter as the central figures. The style is more finished than that encountered in Harley 603, rather less wild; it is perhaps one of the best expressions of this style in an Anglo-Saxon context.

Another lively Winchester manuscript of perhaps slightly later date (c.1050) is a very fine psalter (British Library, Cotton Tiberius C.vi). It is full of drawings and diagrams in brown and red outline with blue and green shading, detail being picked out in orange and red. There are scenes from the life of

231

232

233 Crucifixion, from a psalter
(Paris, Bibliothèque Nationale, lat. 943,
fol. 4v). 31 × 20 cm

234 Crucifixion, from the Sherborne
Pontifical, made at Winchester
(London, British Library, Cotton
Tiberius C.vi, fol. 13r)

David and the life of Christ, musical instruments, diagrams and illuminated 234
miniatures as well as initials. Full of life and highly mobile, the figures show
that even at this late date Anglo-Saxon drawing had not lost its verve.

More than sixty late Anglo-Saxon manuscripts contain drawings and it is
impossible to mention them all here. It is only proper however to mention two
further examples, one because of its subject matter and the other because of its
quality. The first is one of a series of Anglo-Saxon calendars (British Library, 235
Cotton Julius A.vi) and was probably written at Canterbury in the early
eleventh century. It is the earliest illustrated English calendar and depicts
month by month the activities of the countryside from January ploughing to
December threshing. This manuscript may have served as a model for a
painted calendar (British Library, Cotton Tiberius B.v), but is symptomatic of 236, 237
an increasing interest at this period in the illustration of secular subjects such
as astronomy, travel and myth, which sometimes reflect the detail found on
Harley 603 and the Caedmon manuscript.

187

nuuiglanc populi quadrif leo que repaufat
nernif gaudenc petruf paulufque kalendif
Marcialif rxince pridiaf idemque kalendaf

235 Detail from a calendar, probably written at
Canterbury
(London, British Library, Cotton Julius A.vi, fol. 5v)

dia generor Inicianir cornua tauri
maias habet dies xxx i luna xxxi
xi c b mai I acobus merute philippusq micare ibis

236, 237 Detail (*above*) and page (*right*) from a
calendar
(London, British Library, Cotton Tiberius B.v, ff. 5r,
8v). Size of page 26 × 21.7 cm

188

Terminat ar... medio sua sig(n)a december
DECEMBER HABET DIES XXXI LUNA XXX
PRIMA DIES MENSIS KASIANUM CONTINET ALMUM.
Atque secunda dies uictorem possidet aequum.
Tertia crispinum cum magno nomine scm.
Quarta dies retinet prudentem cum quoque eraclo.
Quinta teneo ueram dominam anglor ialhyrisae caram.
Sexta dies reuocat hermonem cumque rogato.
Septima concludit policarpum cum theodoro.
Octaua deprimit urbanum nomine scm.
Bona ualentinum fecundat nomine pulchro.
Decima eulalia congaudet uirgine casta.
Undecima rutulat pastorem rite damascum.
Aduodena dies donata nomine gaudet.
Tres decima rutulat uirgo iam lucia sca.
IAN Denis et nonis uictor dormitq kldis.
Candidus eluxit nonis bis cumquoq fausto.
Atq ualentinus denis sepumq kldis.
Sex decimis martir ignatius sorte kldis.
Sol oriens intrat quinis ter sidera capri.
Bis septem sequitur scs gregorius almus.
Promit anastasius denis trinisq kldis.
Solstitiu thomas habitat in cardine scs.
undecimis rome felix deponitur archus.
cornelius denis eleutheriusq kalendis.
Bonis iam uigiles repetamus pectore xpm.
Octauus felix ...
EPTENIS MARTYR Stephani sangui...
... annis semis superat ...
nfantes qnis uapulant morte kldis.
elice colimus quadris in sorte kldis.
rinis a sedo pausat florentius equis.
iluestrum pridias notum celebrant in orbe.

238 Marginal illustration to Psalm 82,
'make me as on to a wheel', from the
Bury Psalter
(Rome, Vatican, Biblioteca Apostolica,
Reg. lat.12, fol. 90v)

The second manuscript is the so-called Bury Psalter (Vatican, Biblioteca Apostolica, Reg. lat.12), probably written at Canterbury in the second quarter of the eleventh century. This book perhaps provides the most sensitive and skilful use of line drawing by the Anglo-Saxons. Nobody can fail to be fascinated by the conceit of the illustration to Psalm 82 – 'make me as on to a wheel' – or to be impressed by the figures standing in adoration all around one page on folio 73v. Here is all the movement and fluttering sensitivity of the Anglo-Saxon artist who has at last out-shone his model and produced a great work of art.

Figural art in metalwork and sculpture

A number of pieces of metalwork reflect in their ornament the figural style of the Winchester manuscripts. Particularly interesting in this context is a portable altar in the Cluny Museum, Paris. In the centre is a slab of red porphyry but on the silver frame are scenes executed in a linear technique. At the 'top' of the altar (which lay flat) is a Crucifixion between the symbols of St Luke and St John and, below, an *agnus dei* between the symbols of St Matthew and St Mark. On the side panels are figures of the Virgin and St Peter, each placed above an angel. It is difficult to place this object with great accuracy, but in many ways it resembles the style of the *Liber Vitae* of the New Minster at Winchester. Much more stolid are the figures on the Drahmal Cross, in the treasury of St Michael's Cathedral in Brussels, which bears an Old English inscription including the maker's name DRAHMAL ME WORHTE (Drahmal made me) incised on the copper-gilt face. The ends of the cross arms are decorated with the Evangelist symbols, haloed and winged as half-length figures. An inscription on one side records that it was made by two brothers Æthelmær and Adelwold in memory of their brother Ælfric. Other examples of the figural style in metalwork are rare, but are known – for instance on a crozier in the Cologne Cathedral treasury, often attributed to St Heriberht (999–1021).

The sculpture which reflects this brilliant period of art in the south of England is probably best seen in miniature in the walrus ivory carvings which form a surprisingly large body of material. Directly in the tradition of the Benedictional of St Æthelwold is a fragmentary Baptism panel of unknown provenance in the British Museum. The treatment of the clothes of the officiating figure (presumably John the Baptist), the skilful suggestion of water and the slightly hunched back are almost exactly the features portrayed so often in the Benedictional. This ivory is probably of late tenth-century date; it is certainly not later than 1025. Another ivory with iconographic parallels to the Benedictional is in the Liverpool City Museum. It is very closely related to the manuscript; practically all the details are similar, even to the two horned cattle which stand over the Infant in the crib.

The most famous Winchester style ivory is a triangular panel, presumably from the spandrel between two triangular-headed features, from Winchester itself. Although an attempt has recently been made to date it *c*.1100, the form of the clothes (which lack the triangularity of much of the post-Conquest folds) and the general stance of the angels, relate it clearly to the end of the tenth century. Convincing parallels to their stance and overall appearance can be seen in the Charter of the New Minster, where practically every detail is clearly paralleled. The heads are slightly heavier, perhaps, than those in the

239 Portable altar, with crucifixion, angels and evangelists round the border. Length 26.4 cm. (Paris, Musée Cluny)

240 The Drahmal Cross. Height 45.9 cm. (Brussels, Treasury of the Cathedral of St Michael and St Gudule)

241 Walrus ivory panel with two
angels.
7.5 × 5 cm. (London, Victoria and
Albert Museum)

242 Walrus ivory panel showing the Nativity.
8 × 6.5 cm. (Liverpool, Merseyside County Museums)

192

manuscripts, but can be closely compared to other heads on Anglo-Saxon
ivory panels, particularly on a Crucifixion scene from a private collection in
Brussels or even to the heads on the Liverpool ivory.

243–6   A small casket in the Cleveland Museum, which turned up near Uttoxeter,
Staffordshire, in the early years of the nineteenth century, provides a rare
glimpse of a little represented medium. It is made of boxwood, and is the only
major piece of wooden carving of the Anglo-Saxon period with any pretence to
artistic quality. It is of house-shaped form with laid-back gables and is carved
in relief with scenes from the life of Christ. The eyes of some of the figures were
originally inlaid with glass. The scenes include the Nativity, the Baptism of
Christ, the Entry into Jerusalem, the Crucifixion, the Ascension, and Christ in
Glory. It is executed in a slightly ham-fisted version of the Winchester style.
The large heads are ugly and dominate the carving, the draperies rarely have

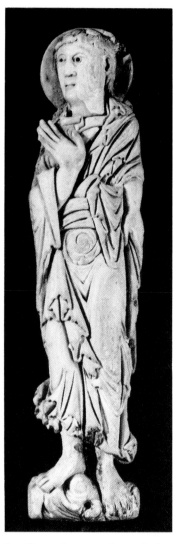

247, 248 Walrus ivory figures of the Virgin and St John
the Evangelist.
Both 12.5 cm high. (Saint Omer, Musée Hôtel Sandelin)

the fluttering quality of the true Winchester style and there is a general
clumsiness of execution. In some elements, however, there are flashes of
quality, particularly in the Ascension scene, where the cloud and the dress of
Christ are truly reminiscent of late tenth-century English painting. Could this
possibly be a product of the West Midlands where it was found?

Returning to the corpus of ivories one is struck by the continuity in this
medium of the inhabited vine-scroll, the finest example of which is to be seen
on the tau (T-shaped) crozier from Alcester, Worcestershire, originally
embellished with gold foil and gems. Here the acanthus ornament of the early
eleventh century is inhabited by occasional animals which are in the direct
Anglo-Saxon tradition. The Ascension scene in the centre of one side is very
close to that on the Reculver stone fragments and perhaps gives one pause for
thought concerning these controversial pieces.

An ivory crucifixion figure in the Victoria and Albert Museum, London, is
set on a metal-cased reliquary in the form of a cross. The metal casing has a
trick of filigree (one strand passing over another) which associates it with
material from the Aachen/Essen area of Germany about the year 1000. The
crucified Christ is, however, one of the most splendid Anglo-Saxon carvings
and must have been put in this setting in Germany. It is closely paralleled by

269

65–8

270

194

the figure of Christ in one of the most moving Anglo-Saxon drawings, the Crucifixion scene in a late tenth-century psalter in the British Library (Harley 2904). A pair of ivories said to have come from the Abbey of Saint Bertin at Saint Omer, depicting the Virgin and St John, has the same ability to move, by means of the exquisite quality of their carving and their expressive faces.

Secular ivory objects are rare at this period, but two seal-dies survive which hint at splendour outside the Church, one (on loan to the British Museum) is of rather coarse quality; but another, found at Wallingford, Berkshire, has a handle on which are carved enthroned figures, perhaps the Two Persons of the Trinity, with their feet on a naked body. It has a seal-die on both sides. One die is carved in intaglio and depicts the seated figure of a woman in flowing Winchester style draperies, with her name, Godgytha. The reverse of this seal is carved in imitation of a coin of Harthacnut for a man named Godwine, presumably in the period after 1042, when that particular type of coin was current. The style of the draperies on the figure of Godgytha belongs to the first half of the eleventh century rather than to the post-Harthacnut period.

Stone sculpture

Stone sculpture of this period is rarely found in the south of England, but over the last twenty years the corpus has increased through excavation. Much of the material is of poor quality or is simple architectural embellishment, much of it is difficult to date and only rarely is material found with unequivocally datable ornament. What survives is often of second- or even third-rate quality and, when compared with the courtly manuscripts and ivory carvings (even with the metalwork), can be seen as such. Little survives from the major centres of the tenth-century reform movement. Bradford-on-Avon and Codford St Peter, both in Wiltshire, and Winchester and Gloucester, are among the few places where sculptural pieces of real quality which can be dated to the tenth and eleventh centuries are found, apart from a small group of stones decorated in the Scandinavian taste to which I shall return. Yet sculpture reflects the sequence of late Anglo-Saxon art; consider, for example, the balanced, if rather incompetent, inhabited plant-scrolls on a stone from the New Examination Schools, Oxford, which can be compared (if only very generally) with the inhabited scroll on the frontispiece of the Corpus Christi Bede. A closer comparison to the same manuscript is the symmetrical plant-scroll on the recently found stone fragment from the excavations at St Oswald's Priory, Gloucester, which is a highly competent piece of carving. The leaves are beautifully faceted and the axial design is not far away from that found on the lid of the ivory pen-case in the British Museum. Similar axial plant-scrolls are encountered elsewhere, at Braunton in Devon, on a recently excavated stone from Wells in Somerset and on one of the stones incorporated (?re-used) in the eleventh-century tower of the church at Barnack, Northamptonshire.

The stone from Codford St Peter is in the long tradition of English standing crosses (although only one face survives complete); it portrays a man plucking fruit from a tree. This is a highly competent piece of carving characterized by Kendrick as 'English in its hard and robust vivacity and in its tense abstraction; it is a stylistic precursor of the later Winchester art, and a pregnant testimony to the existence of some inexplicable but long-lasting aesthetic instinct in Wessex'. Kendrick was evidently fascinated by this piece which he saw as the only real counterpart to the fine carving of the immediately pre-Scandinavian

249 Drawing of stone with inhabited plant-scrolls, from the New Examination Schools, Oxford. Length about 78 cm. (Oxford, Ashmolean Museum)

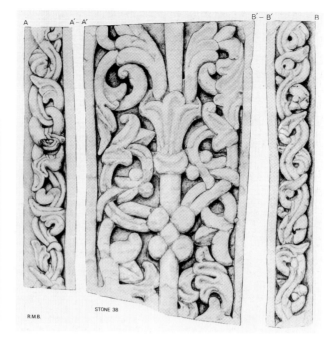

251 *Right*: inhabited plant-scrolls on a stone fragment from St Oswald's Priory, Gloucester (Gloucester City Museum and Art Gallery)

250 Stone with plant-scrolls on the tower of the parish church at Barnack, Northamptonshire

sculpture of the north of England. He attributed it to the middle of the ninth century but was clearly uncomfortable with this dating, as is shown by his reference to the Winchester style. It seems logical to follow Talbot Rice and place it in close relationship to the mainstream Winchester manuscripts, to compare the light-footed stance of the man (as indeed Kendrick did) to the stance of the king in the New Minster Charter or perhaps (for the sense of movement is similar) to the sides of the ivory pen-case discussed above. It is unfortunately a unique representative of an otherwise unknown school of sculpture, but we should be bold and place it firmly in the tenth century – and perhaps quite late in that century.

261

True Winchester figures are, however, best seen in two flying angels, now set high up in a secondary position in the east wall of the little church of St Lawrence at Bradford-on-Avon. Presumably derived from a great Crucifixion, they exhibit many of the features of the angels which hold the mandorla in the New Minster Charter, although, perhaps because of the medium, the drapery is less fluttery. These again must date from the second half of the tenth century and may be compared with some confidence to the angels on the triangular plaque from Winchester. These angels are in the mainstream of Winchester art, a fact clearly demonstrated if they are compared to the angel from Winterbourne Steepleton, Dorset, which is a poor version of the same subject and consequently difficult to date (Talbot Rice dated it '*c*.910' – a remarkably precise statement – and Kendrick eventually admitted defeat and placed it in the Norman period). The lack of sculpture of this period in the south of England and its poor general quality make the most rational and painstaking scholar give up any dating attempt. Many of the large Crucifixion figures found in southern English churches have been treated in this manner, but that from Romsey, Hampshire, is more distinctive and George Zarnecki has drawn convincing parallels between it and a group of Carolingian ivories. A trace of the Winchester style may perhaps be recognized on this piece in the hand of God as it reaches out of the cloud, but little else on the Romsey rood is susceptible of stylistic analysis.

253, 254

255

257

196

253, 254 Two angels in St Lawrence, Bradford-on-
Avon, Wiltshire.
Length of each 1.52 m

255 Angel on the exterior of St Michael, Winterbourne
Steepleton, Dorset

252 *Left*: carved stone at the parish church of Codford
St Peter, Wiltshire, showing a man plucking fruit from a
tree.
Height *c*.1.25 m

257 The hand of God.
Detail of a Crucifixion at Romsey
Abbey, Hampshire

256 Grave-marker, from the Old
Minster, Winchester.
Height 66 cm. (Winchester Cathedral)

256   From Winchester itself, from excavations in the eastern crypt of the Old
Minster, comes an upright grave-marker carved in the true Winchester style.
Carved in deep relief it represents a tripartite arcade within which curtains are
drawn to reveal what might be a hanging lamp. The curtains are carved with
great precision in a slightly stiff version of normal Winchester draperies.

258   From the same place at Winchester came a tantalizing fragment of figural
sculpture which has been much discussed in the twenty years since it was
found. Part of a frieze, it shows in relief a striding warrior wearing a suit of
chain mail. His head and chest are missing; behind him is a prostrate figure (of
which only head, shoulders and arm survive) below the head and crossed legs
of an animal, whose tongue passes into the mouth of the man. The stone forms
part of a frieze which the excavator says was destroyed when the Old Minster
was demolished in 1093–4; it is interpreted as part of the structure of that
building. The scene depicting the fallen warrior has been associated with a

198

258 Part of a frieze from the Old
Minster, Winchester.
Width 53 cm. (Winchester Cathedral)

259 Cross-head from Durham.
Height 66 cm. (Durham Cathedral)

260 Coped grave-cover from Durham.
Surviving length 1.4 m. (Durham
Cathedral)

199

reference to an incident in *Volsunga Saga*, where Sigmund escapes by pulling out a wolf's tongue. There has been some scepticism about this interpretation but nobody has produced a better explanation; the further suggestion that such a scene would be appropriate in the burial chamber of Knut (who could claim descent from Sigmund) appears a very thin argument when we remember that Knut was intent on becoming a Christian king and would probably not want to advertise his pagan ancestry. There is a spurious

277

similarity between this stone and the art of the Bayeux Tapestry, which is dependent entirely on the position and shape of the sword and the form of the mail shirt (actually represented by a chequer pattern at Winchester and not, as at Bayeux, by interlocking rings); other details, the hair of the prone man for example, are, however, not paralleled in the tapestry and, although we might here have a narrative not unlike that depicted at Bayeux, any comparison must be made with great care. The stone has recently been claimed as Romanesque and this seems a happy solution.

It has been mentioned above (p. 152) that there is little or no trace of the Winchester style in northern English sculpture. The major datable ecclesiastical site of the North in the late Anglo-Saxon period is Durham which was founded as the ultimate successor to Lindisfarne in 995. There is no evidence that there was a church in Durham before the Community of St Cuthbert finally settled there, but the St Oswald's Cross would indicate that this was the case; indeed it would be very strange if there was no cell of Lindisfarne here before the monks moved from Chester-le-Street. The St Oswald's Cross, which is certainly of early tenth-century date, need not concern us here; but a series of sculptures, which while not very accomplished are not uninteresting, was found in the foundations of the present cathedral.

259

These include a number of cross-heads with very elaborate iconography executed in a crude style which has no clear diagnostic features. Assuming that the sculpture post-dates 995 it is extremely old-fashioned (as witness the interlaced ribbon-like animals on one of the arms). Similar old-fashioned

260

ornament is to be seen on a tombstone of rather more up-to-date form, where the surface is decorated with highly competent interlace of good tenth-century tradition. Unfortunately no clearly coherent story can be erected to tell of non-Scandinavian influences in northern England in the late tenth and early eleventh century. Such a statement is true not only for sculpture, but also for manuscript art (almost totally missing) and metalwork (strangely missing in the archaeological record).

The last of the Scandinavians

From 980 onwards the whole of England was subject to attack, first from the Norwegians and later from the Danes. The Scandinavians came to England for loot and they got it in the form of massive payments of silver – the Danegeld – which were given to them as bribes to leave the country. But once having paid the geld the country was open to further attack and it was only with the conquest of England by the Danish king Knut that the country was relieved (gradually) of this tax. Knut became king in 1017 and, until the death of Harthacnut in 1042, a Danish dynasty ruled the country. This political situation influenced English art, for a handful of objects were produced here which are decorated in the style – the Ringerike style – then current in Scandinavia.

261 *Opposite*: King Edgar, flanked by the Virgin and St Peter, offers the Charter of the New Minster, Winchester, to Christ (London, British Library, Cotton Vespasian A.viii, fol. 2v). 28.8 × 16.2 cm. See p. 174

262 Portrait and symbol of St Luke, from the Judith of Flanders Gospels (New York, Pierpont Morgan Library, M.709, fol. 48v). 29.5 × 19 cm. See p. 174

263 Canon tables from the Bury Gospels (London, British Library, Harley 76, fol. 8v). 26.5 × 20 cm. See p. 176

264 Portrait and symbol of
St John, from the Grimbald
Gospels
(London, British Library,
Add. 34890, fol. 114v).
32 × 24.5 cm.
See pp. 174, 176

265 The Deposition, from
the Sacramentary of Robert
of Jumièges
(Rouen, Bibliothèque
municipale, Y.6 (274), fol.
72r). 34 × 22 cm.
See p. 174

266 Walrus ivory carving of the Baptism of Christ.
Height 9 cm (London, British Museum). See p. 190

270 *Right*: figure of the crucified Christ, in walrus ivory, set on a later cross-shaped reliquary made in Germany.
Height of cross 18.5 cm (London, Victoria and Albert Museum). See p. 194

267, 268 Front and back of Godwine's seal, found at Wallingford, Berkshire.
Height 8.5 cm (London, British Museum). See p. 195

269 Walrus ivory crozier-head from Alcester, Warwickshire.
Length 14.5 cm (London, British Museum). See p. 194

271–3 *Opposite*: three works that show the influence of Scandinavian art in England.
Top: stone panel showing a large animal caught in the coils of a serpent – a coloured drawing which brings out the faded colours of the original; width 57 cm (Museum of London). *Below left*: copper-gilt brooch from Pitney, Somerset; diameter 3.9 cm (London, British Museum). *Below right*: a bone belt-slide from the River Thames at London, with the image of a man, head missing; diameter 6 cm (London, British Museum). See p. 209

274 Stone slab in Otley parish church, Yorkshire

275 Copper-gilt strip with foliate ornament, from Winchester.
29 × 4.5 cm. (Winchester Cathedral Library)

Chief among English objects decorated in the Ringerike style is a stone panel from the neighbourhood of St Paul's churchyard in London. An inscription on the side of the stone in Scandinavian runic characters reads 'Ginna and Toki had this stone set up'. The carving represents a large striding beast, caught in the tendril-like coils of a serpent. The surface of the stone was painted on a gesso-like surface with two main colours: a brownish-red for the snake and some details of the great beast, and black for the body of the animal. The body of the animal was painted with white spots. London has produced a number of Ringerike style objects: another stone possibly from St Paul's, a fragmentary stone from All-Hallows-by-the-Tower and a number of metal and bone objects.

In many ways the Ringerike style chimes with the more ragged acanthus ornament of the Winchester style. (It can be no accident for example that a purely Ringerike foliate ornament appears on a copper-gilt strip from Winchester itself.) Indeed, it is interesting to see the Ringerike style appear in two or three Winchester style manuscripts alongside English forms. In Cambridge University Library Ff.I.23 (probably from the Abbey of Winchcombe), for example, are several initials which are purely Ringerike in form. The letter d illustrated here has the pear-shaped eye, the lip-lappet and the elongated tendrils typical of the style. Other manuscripts exhibit traits of the Ringerike style, including the Caedmon Bible (Oxford, Bodleian Library, Junius 11). Such occurrences are, however, rare and, although a fair number of other examples of Ringerike style on stone, bone and metal are found in southern England, the style never took firm root here. Indeed in the north of England (where one would expect a more easy reception of the style) it is even rarer; the Otley Stone is one of the few examples definitely made in the North.

It should, however, be pointed out that the Ringerike style was close to the taste of the Anglo-Saxons. The style in its native Scandinavia had roots in

276 Initial d from the so-called Winchcombe Psalter (Cambridge, University Library, Ff.I.23, fol. 37v)

Anglo-Saxon and Ottonian art; it was from these sources that it drew such features as the tendril and tri-lobate features which are such an important element in its make-up, and it may well be that the traffic of manuscripts to Scandinavia as it became more and more Christian fuelled the development of the style. What we see in the St Paul's stone and the Cambridge manuscript is a backwash from the area where the style developed to its original area of inspiration during the reign in England of a Danish king, Knut the Great.

The effect of the Norman Conquest

There are difficulties in separating Anglo-Saxon and Norman art. Although the Conquest of 1066 was a political watershed, Francis Wormald and others have clearly demonstrated that the Norman Conquest caused no hiatus in the Anglo-Saxon ornamental traditions. The Normans who came to England reformed the Church, but they reformed it with clerics from Normandy whose artistic taste had been very much affected by English influences in the art of their homeland. This is particularly seen in the manuscript art of Normandy which in the early eleventh century was full of Anglo-Saxon elements. Architectural sculpture was little affected by Anglo-Saxon styles; any traceable influences came through the manuscripts. True Norman architecture as found at Bernay, Dijon or Jumièges was little affected by English stylistic traits: indeed, Norman Romanesque architecture soon submerged the English architectural tradition, a fact clearly demonstrated by the greatest mid-eleventh-century English church, Edward the Confessor's Westminster Abbey, which was modelled on the nearly completed Norman Abbey of Jumièges, a masterpiece of the true Romanesque. There is little Romanesque taste in pre-Conquest Anglo-Saxon art. Although Dodwell has identified such elements in British Library Harley 603, in British Library Cotton Tiberius C.vi and so on – more perhaps at Winchester than Canterbury – he has, however, wisely said that

> the immediate effect of the Conquest was not to accelerate the Romanesque development, but rather to impede it: the Norman figure style that was introduced, and even at first the accompanying figure style of native Anglo-Saxon artists, were both reactionary.

277 This is demonstrated in the most extraordinary propaganda document of Norman history, the Bayeux Tapestry. Although produced for Norman patrons to tell of the justice of the Norman conquest of England, it was almost certainly made in Canterbury in the Anglo-Saxon style. The case that it was made in England is strengthened by inscriptional as well as stylistic evidence. It has many archaic elements in its ornament but was almost certainly made to the order of Bishop Odo of Bayeux before his disgrace in 1082. It is a highly sophisticated wool embroidery worked on a plain linen background and executed in laid and couched work with stem and outline stitches (it survives to a length of 69.55 m and is 50 cm broad). It depicts the events leading up to the defeat of Harold at Hastings in lively detail. There are many incidental scenes in the borders, some of which are merely ornamental, others telling a story. The tapestry lies outside the framework of this book but it is of interest in that it is the only surviving example of its kind – that others were produced in the Anglo-Saxon period is known from the literary record. Once again we may marvel at the skill of the Anglo-Saxon needlewoman.

271

Anglo-Saxon sculpture of the immediate pre-Conquest period was, as we have seen, pretty poor stuff. Modest, unassuming and derivative, it stands in stark contrast to the manuscript art. Only in the stone from St Paul's Cathedral does one feel any lifting of the spirit. The tradition of Ruthwell, of Breedon and of Wolverhampton had disappeared and the way was paved for the introduction into English sculpture of elements which had their origin in the great Romanesque churches of Normandy – Bayeux, Caen and Rucqueville. In George Zarnecki's words concerning the sculpture of Normandy at the time of the Conquest '[it] had a certain naive quality, but it did not lack strength or vigour'. It was not, however, easily acceptable to an English palate accustomed to the weak, stale quality of pre-Conquest sculpture. The Anglo-Saxon craftsman clung on to his own ideas with unfortunate results, for when traces of the Anglo-Saxon style do appear in post-Conquest sculpture (as on the Ely capitals of about 1090) the details are weak and flat or (as on the Southwell, Nottinghamshire, and Water Stratford, Buckinghamshire, tympana of the early twelfth century) archaic and naïve. There was an undoubted resistance to Romanesque sculpture in eleventh-century England, a resistance which resulted in a style which inhibited the development of sculpture in the newly-conquered land.

The English traditions did, however, survive with some vitality after the Conquest in the manuscript art. Perhaps it was the inherent English love of caricature which helped the process. Certainly the English taste for twisted animals is seen in such metal masterpieces as the Gloucester candle-stick, or perhaps more modestly and satisfyingly in the adoption of the ultimate Viking style – the Urnes style – which was introduced into England, perhaps from Ireland through the Bristol Channel trade route from Dublin, towards the end of the eleventh century. It is seen at its best in the sinuous snake-like bodies of the fighting beasts on the Pitney Brooch, an Urnes style object made in England towards the end of the eleventh century. In this object we return again to the tradition of Germanic animal art which has run, a *Leitmotiv*, throughout this book.

272

277 Detail from the Bayeux Tapestry, showing the English (on a hill) being attacked by Norman cavalry at the Battle of Hastings.
Height 50 cm. (Bayeux, Musée de la Tapisserie de Bayeux)

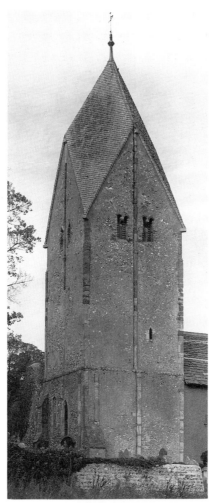

Anglo-Saxon churches, the setting for many of the works covered in this book, have suffered harshly from the passage of time. Although no major building has survived intact, a fair number of English churches have Anglo-Saxon features (mostly identifiable by the style of their towers, arches and windows).

279 St Mary, Sompting, Sussex. The tower roof, which is probably of post-Conquest date, belongs to a type familiar in Germany and known as a 'Rhenish helm'. It is seen in miniature in the tenth-century censer cover shown in pl. 209

281 *Right*: All Saints, Earls Barton, Northamptonshire. The tower and chancel arch are all that survive of this church; the eastern quoins show that the nave was narrower than the tower. The pilaster strips, the quoins executed in 'long and short' work (corners formed of stones placed alternately vertically and horizontally) and the baluster window-shafts are all characteristic Anglo-Saxon features. It dates from the early eleventh century

278 St Peter, Monkwearmouth, Co. Durham. Begun and finished in 674. Of the original church only the foundations of the nave, the western porch (the lower portion of the tower in this picture) and part of the western wall survive

280 St Lawrence, Bradford-on-Avon, Wiltshire, a small church of the eleventh century whose structure survived by being incorporated into a later building. It is a two-cell church; to the left is the tall narrow nave; to the right the chancel. The door originally opened into a south porticus – a corresponding one on the north survives. Two carved angels from the interior are shown in pls. 253, 254

282 Triangular-headed openings from the tower into the nave of St Mary's church, Deerhurst, Gloucestershire. Probably mid-tenth century

283 One of the most imposing churches of the late Anglo-Saxon period is St Mary, Stow, Lincolnshire. It was probably built in the mid-eleventh century. The great crossing arches belong to this period, but the effect is slightly obscured by the fourteenth-century arches built inside the Anglo-Saxon ones

284 Arch into the tower of St Bene't, Cambridge.
Eleventh century. The tower was perhaps capped like
Sompting, pl. 279. The two animals at the springing of
the arch contrast with the distantly classical style
of the rest

285 St Nicholas, Worth, Sussex:
an eleventh-century church whose basic structure has
survived in spite of drastic restoration. Here we are
looking through the chancel arch, with its semi-circular
respond and cushion capital, towards the narrower arch
of the north transept

Sources

As this is a book of synthesis, much of the material has been published previously. The following list of books and papers, given by chapter and page number, is selective. It is intended to lead the reader to a major publication of an object or of an idea. There is inevitably some repetition, but the references should be a natural starting-point for a student's own investigations into a particular problem. General select bibliographies referring to the whole book and, where appropriate, to the whole of a chapter are also provided and these should be consulted if there is no immediate reference against a page number.

General

J. J. G. Alexander, *Insular manuscripts 6th to the 9th century*, London 1978.

J. Beckwith, *Ivory carvings in early medieval England*, London 1972.

British Academy corpus of Anglo-Saxon stone sculpture (various authors; general editor R. Cramp), London 1984–.

J. Brøndsted, *Early English ornament*, Copenhagen/London 1924.

W. G. Collingwood, *Northumbrian crosses of the pre-Norman age*, London 1927.

E. Fernie, *The architecture of the Anglo-Saxons*, London 1983.

D. A. Hinton, *Catalogue of the Anglo-Saxon ornamental metalwork 700–1100 in the . . . Ashmolean Museum*, Oxford 1974.

T. D. Kendrick, *Anglo-Saxon art to A.D. 900*, London 1938.

T. D. Kendrick, *Late Saxon and Viking art*, London 1949.

O. Lehmann-Brockhaus, *Lateinische Schriftquellen zur Kunst in England Wales und Schottland vom Jahre 901 bis zum Jahre 1307*, Munich 1955–60.

M. Rickert, *Painting in Britain: the Middle Ages*, London 1954.

E. Temple, *Anglo-Saxon manuscripts 900–1066*, London 1976.

D. M. Wilson, *Anglo-Saxon ornamental metalwork, 700–1100, in the British Museum*, London 1964.

E. Wilson, *Early medieval designs from Britain* (British Museum Pattern Books), London 1983.

Chapter 1: Taste, personalities and survival

R. Bruce-Mitford, *The Sutton Hoo ship burial*, London 1975–83.

C. R. Dodwell, *Anglo-Saxon art, a new perspective*, Manchester 1982.

9 C. R. Dodwell, 'Losses of Anglo-Saxon art in the Middle Ages', *Bulletin of the John Rylands University Library of Manchester* lvi (1973–4), 74–92.

10 J. J. G. Alexander, 'Some aesthetic principles in the use of colour in Anglo-Saxon art', *Anglo-Saxon England* iv (1975), 145–54.

10 B. Colgrave and R. A. B. Mynors (eds.), *Bede's ecclesiastical history of the English people*, Oxford 1969.

10 R. Gem and P. Tudor-Craig, 'A "Winchester School" wall-painting at Nether Wallop, Hampshire', *Anglo-Saxon England* ix (1980), 115–36.

11 E. Crowfoot and S. C. Hawkes, 'Early Anglo-Saxon gold braids', *Medieval Archaeology* xi (1967), 42–86.

13 R. J. Cramp, 'Monastic sites', *The archaeology of Anglo-Saxon England* (ed. D. M. Wilson), London 1976, 201–52.

14–15 *The Vikings in England and in their Danish homeland* (Exhibition catalogue Copenhagen/Århus/York), London 1981.

16 V. I. Evison, 'The body in the ship at Sutton Hoo', *Anglo-Saxon studies* i (1979), 121–38.

26 B. Salin, *Die altgermanische Thierornamentik*, Stockholm 1904.

Chapter 2: The seventh-century explosion

R. T. Farrell (ed.), *Bede and Anglo-Saxon England*, Oxford 1978.

E. A. Lowe, *Codices Latini Antiquiores*, Oxford 1934–71.

F. Masai, *Essai sur les origines de la miniature dite irlandaise*, Brussels 1947.

C. Nordenfalk, *Celtic and Anglo-Saxon painting*, London 1977.

29 C. F. Battiscombe (ed.), *The relics of St Cuthbert*, Oxford 1956.

29 C. E. Wright, 'The dispersal of the monastic libraries and the beginning of Anglo-Saxon studies', *Cambridge Biographical Society* iii (1951), 208–37.

29 F. Wormald, *The miniatures in the Gospels of St Augustine*, Cambridge 1954.

30 T. J. Brown (ed.), *The Stonyhurst Gospel of St John*, London 1959.

30 E. A. Lowe, *English uncial*, Oxford 1960.

32–49 T. D. Kendrick *et al.*, *Evangeliorum Quattuor Codex Lindisfarnensis*, Olten and Lausanne 1956–60.

33 A. A. Luce *et al.*, *Evangeliorum*

Quattuor Codex Durmachensis, Olten and Lausanne 1960.

34 M. Schapiro, 'The miniatures of the Florence Diatesseron', *Art Bulletin* iv (1973), 494–531.

34 R. B. K. Stevenson, 'Sculpture in Scotland in the 6th–9th centuries A.D.', *Kolloquium über spätantike und frühmittelalterliche Skulptur* ii (ed. V. Milojčić), Mainz 1971, 65–74.

34 I. Henderson, 'Pictish art and the Book of Kells', *Ireland in Early Medieval Europe* (ed. D. Whitelock, R. McKitterick and D. Dumville), Cambridge 1982, 79–105.

36 J. Backhouse, *The Lindisfarne Gospels*, London 1981.

36 C. D. Verey, T. J. Brown and E. Coatsworth (eds.), *The Durham Gospels* (Early English manuscripts in facsimile xx), Copenhagen 1980.

49 R. L. S. Bruce-Mitford, 'The art of the Codex Amiatinus', *Journal of the British Archaeological Association*, 1969, 1–25.

49 P.-J. Nordhagen, *The Codex Amiatinus and the Byzantine element in the Northumbrian renaissance* (Jarrow lecture 1977).

49–50 C. F. Battiscombe, *The relics of St Cuthbert*, Oxford 1956.

50–56 R. Cramp, *Early Northumbrian sculpture* (Jarrow lecture 1965).

50–53 R. Cramp, 'Early Northumbrian sculpture at Hexham', *Saint Wilfrid at Hexham* (ed. D. P. Kirby), Newcastle upon Tyne 1974, 115–40.

50–56 R. Cramp, 'The Anglian tradition in the ninth century', *Anglo-Saxon and Viking Age sculpture* (ed. J. Lang), Oxford 1978, 1–32.

54–5 H. M. and J. Taylor, *Anglo-Saxon architecture* i–ii, Cambridge 1965.

Chapter 3: The eighth and ninth centuries

59 P. Godman (ed.), *Alcuin, the bishops, kings and saints of York*, Oxford 1982.

60–61 See Chapter 4.

61–3 R. N. Bailey, *The Durham Cassiodorus* (Jarrow lecture 1978).

61–3 Idem, 'Bede's text of Cassiodorus' commentary on the psalms', *The Journal of Theological Studies* xxxiv, i (1983), 189–93.

63 P. Meyvaert, *Bede and Gregory the Great* (Jarrow lecture 1974).

63 O. Arngart, *The Leningrad Bede* (Early English manuscripts in facsimile ii), Copenhagen 1952.

63 D. H. Wright, 'The date of the Leningrad Bede', *Revue Benedictine* lxxi (1961), 265–86.

63 M. Schapiro, *Late Antique, early Christian and medieval art, selected papers*, London 1980. ('The decoration of the Leningrad manuscript of Bede', 199–224.)

64 E. Bakka, 'Some English decorated metal objects found in Norwegian Viking graves', *Årbok for Universitetet i Bergen, humanistisk serie*, 1963, no. 1.

67 D. Tweddle, 'The Coppergate Helmet', *Fornvännen* lxxviii (1983), 105–112.

70 W. O. Stevens, T. D. Hill, A. S. Cook and R. T. Farrell, *The Anglo-Saxon cross*, Hamden 1977.

71 W. G. Collingwood, articles in *Yorkshire Archaeological Journal*, 1907, 1911 and 1915.

71 W. S. Calverley, *Early sculptured crosses . . . in the present diocese of Carlisle*, Kendal 1899.

71 G. Baldwin Brown, *The arts in early England* vi, part 2 (*Anglo-Saxon sculpture*), London 1937.

71 F. J. Haverfield and W. Greenwell, *A catalogue of the sculptured and inscribed stones in the Cathedral Library, Durham*, Durham 1899.

71 R. Cramp, 'The Anglian tradition in the ninth century', *Anglo-Saxon and Viking Age sculpture* (ed. J. Lang), Oxford 1978, 1–32.

71 R. L. Kozodoy, *The Reculver Cross*, Columbia University Ph.D., 1976.

71 D. Tweddle, 'Anglo-Saxon sculpture in south-east England before *c.*950', *Studies in medieval sculpture* (ed. F. H. Thompson), London 1983, 18–40.

71 D. Talbot Rice, *English art 871–1100*, Oxford 1952.

72 F. Saxl, 'The Ruthwell Cross', *Journal of the Warburg and Courtauld Institutes* vi (1943), 1–19.

72 D. R. Howlett, 'Two panels on the Ruthwell Cross', *Journal of the Warburg and Courtauld Institutes* xxxvii (1974), 333–6.

72 R. I. Page, 'The Bewcastle Cross', *Nottingham medieval studies* iv (1960), 36–57.

72 R. T. Farrell, 'The Archer and associated figures on the Ruthwell Cross – a reconsideration', *Bede and Anglo-Saxon England* (ed. R. T. Farrell) (British Archaeological Reports xlvi), 1978, 96–117.

75–7 R. Cramp, 'The position of the Otley crosses in English sculpture of the eighth and ninth century', *Kolloquium über spätantike und frühmittelalterliche Skulptur* ii, Mainz 1971, 55–65.

80–85 R. Cramp, 'Schools of Mercian sculpture', *Mercian studies* (ed. A.

Dornier), Leicester 1977, 191–234.

80–85 R. A. Smith, 'Examples of Anglian Art', *Archaeologia* lxxiv (1925), 233–54.

85 R. W. P. Cockerton, 'The Wirksworth slab', *Derbyshire Archaeological Journal* lxxxii (1962), 1–20.

85–6 L. E. Webster, 'Stylistic aspects of the Franks Casket', *The Vikings* (ed. R. T. Farrell), 1982, 20–31.

86 B. Green, 'An Anglo-Saxon bone plaque from Larling, Norfolk', *The Antiquaries Journal* li (1971), 321–3.

87–8 W. A. Stein, *The Lichfield Gospels*, University of California, Berkeley, Ph.D., 1980.

91 D. H. Wright (ed.), *The Vespasian Psalter* (Early English manuscripts in facsimile xiv), Copenhagen 1967.

91 H. Wheeler, 'Aspects of Mercian art: the Book of Cerne', *Mercian studies* (ed. A. Dornier), Leicester 1977, 235–44.

94–6 D. M. Wilson and C. E. Blunt, 'The Trewhiddle hoard', *Archaeologia* xcviii (1961), 75–122.

105 M. Longhurst, 'The Easby Cross', *Archaeologia* lxxxi (1931), 43–7.

105 R. Cramp and R. Miket, *Catalogue of the Anglo-Saxon and Viking antiquities in the Museum of Antiquities, Newcastle upon Tyne*, Newcastle upon Tyne 1982.

105 R. Cramp, 'The position of the Otley crosses . . .' (see note to pp. 75–7). *Idem*, 'Schools of Mercian sculpture . . .' (see note to pp. 80–85).

106 D. Tweddle, 'Anglo-Saxon sculpture in south-east England . . .' (see note to p. 71).

106 M. Calberg, 'Tissus et broderies attribués aux saintes Harlinde et Relinde', *Bulletin de la société royale d'archéologie de Bruxelles* (October 1951), 1–26.

110 R. L. S. Bruce-Mitford, 'Late Saxon disc brooches', *Dark-Age Britain* (ed. D. B. Harden), London 1956, 171–201.

110–11 J. R. Clarke, *The Alfred and Minster Lovell jewels* (2nd ed.), Oxford 1961.

110–11 D. R. Howlett, 'The iconography of the Alfred Jewel', *Oxoniensia* xxxix (1974), 44–52.

110–11 E. Bakka, 'The Alfred Jewel and sight', *The Antiquaries Journal* xlvi (1966), 277–82.

111 L. E. Webster, 'An Anglo-Saxon plaque with the symbol of St John the Evangelist', *British Museum occasional paper* x (1980), 11–14.

111 *The Vikings in England and in their Danish homeland* (Exhibition catalogue Copenhagen/Århus/York), London 1981.

Chapter 4: Influences

113–20 D. M. Wilson, 'The art and archaeology of Bedan Northumbria', *Bede and Anglo-Saxon England* (ed. R. T. Farrell) (British Archaeological Reports xlvi), Oxford 1978, 1–22.

114–20 F. T. Wainwright (ed.), *The problem of the Picts*, Edinburgh 1955.

114–20 I. Henderson, *The Picts*, London 1967.

114–20 R. R. Allen and J. Anderson, *The early Christian monuments of Scotland*, Edinburgh 1903.

116 I. Henderson, 'The meaning of the Pictish symbol stones', *The Dark Ages in the Highlands* (Inverness Field Club c.1971), 53–68.

116 *Idem*, 'Pictish art and the Book of Kells', *Ireland in Early Medieval Europe* (ed. D. Whitelock, R. McKitterick and D. Dumville), Cambridge 1982, 79–105.

117 R. B. K. Stevenson, 'Sculpture in Scotland in the 6th–9th centuries A.D.', *Kolloquium über spätantike und frühmittelalterliche Skulptur* ii (ed. V. Milojčić), Mainz 1971, 65–74.

117 I. Henderson, 'Pictish vine-scroll ornament', *From the Stone Age to the 'Forty-Five* (ed. A. O'Connor and D. V. Clarke), Edinburgh 1983, 243–68.

117 F. S. Scott, 'The Hildithryth and the other Hartlepool name-stones', *Archaeologia Aeliana* 4th ser. xxxiv (1956), 196–201.

117–18 A. Small, C. Thomas and D. M. Wilson, *St Ninian's Isle and its treasure*, Oxford 1973.

118 R. Cramp, 'The Anglian sculptured crosses of Dumfriesshire', *Transactions of the Dumfriesshire and Galloway Natural History and Antiquarian Society* xxxvii (1959–60), 9–20.

118–19 *Iona; Argyll, an inventory of the monuments* iv (The Royal Commission on the Ancient and Historical Monuments of Scotland), Edinburgh 1982.

118 W. N. Robertson, 'St John's Cross, Iona, Argyll', *Proceedings of the Society of Antiquaries of Scotland* cvi (1974–5), 111–23.

119 R. B. K. Stevenson, 'The chronology and relationship of some Irish and Scottish crosses', *Journal of the Royal Society of Antiquaries of Ireland* lxxxvi (1956), 84–96.

120–30 F. Henry, *Irish art in the Early Christian period to A.D. 800*, London 1965.

120–30 *Idem, Irish art during the Viking invasions (800–1020 A.D.)*, London 1967.

120–30 *Treasures of early Irish art 1500 B.C. to 1500 A.D.* (ed. P. Crone), New York 1977.

120 M. Ryan (ed.), *The Derrynaflan hoard; a preliminary account*, Dublin 1983.

129 N. Whitfield, 'The finding of the Tara Brooch', *Journal of the Royal Society of Antiquaries of Ireland* civ (1974), 120–42.

129 R. B. K. Stevenson, 'The Hunterston brooch and its significance', *Medieval Archaeology* xviii (1974), 16–42.

129–30 E. H. Alton and P. Meyer, *Evangeliorum Quattuor Codex Cennanensis*, Olten/Lausanne 1951.

129–30 F. Henry, *The Book of Kells*, London 1974.

129 J. Brown, 'Northumbria and the Book of Kells', *Anglo-Saxon England* i (1972), 219–46.

130–38 J. Hubert, J. Porcher, W. F. Volbach, *Carolingian art*, London 1970.

130–38 C. R. Dodwell, *Painting in Europe, 800–1200*, London 1971.

130–38 P. Lasko, *Ars Sacra 800–1200*, London 1972.

131 D. M. Wilson, 'An Anglo-Saxon bookbinding at Fulda (Codex Bonifatianus I)', *The Antiquaries Journal* xli (1961), 199–217.

132 F. Wormald, *The Utrecht Psalter*, Utrecht 1953.

133–7 *Karl der Grosse, Werk und Wirkung*, (exhibition catalogue) Aachen 1965.

135–7 G. Haseloff, *Der Tassilokelch*, Munich 1951.

135–7 J. Werner, 'Frühkarolingische Silberohrringe von Rastede (Oldenburg)', *Germania* xxxvii (1959), 179–92.

135–7 D. M. Wilson, 'The Fejø cup', *Acta Archaeologica* xxxi (1960), 147–73.

138–9 D. M. Wilson and O. Klindt-Jensen, *Viking art*, London 1966.

Chapter 5: From Alfred to the Conquest
R. Deshman, 'Anglo-Saxon art after Alfred', *The Art Bulletin* lvi (1974), 176–200.

D. Talbot Rice, *English art 871–1100*, Oxford 1952.

141–2 S. Keynes and M. Lapidge, *Alfred the Great*, Harmondsworth 1983.

142–50 D. M. Wilson and O. Klindt-Jensen, *Viking art*, London 1966.

142–50 J. Lang (ed.), *Anglo-Saxon and Viking Age sculpture* (British Archaeological Reports 49), Oxford 1978.

142–50 J. Graham-Campbell and D. Kidd, *The Vikings*, London 1980.

142–50 *The Vikings in England and in their Danish homeland* (Exhibition catalogue Copenhagen/Århus/York), London 1981.

142–52 R. N. Bailey, *Viking sculpture in Northern England*, London 1980.

142–52 J. Lang, 'Recent studies in the pre-Conquest sculpture in Northumbria', *Studies in medieval sculpture* (ed. F. T. Thompson), London 1983, 177–89.

143 C. A. Parker, *The ancient crosses at Gosforth, Cumberland*, London 1896.

143–5 J. T. Lang, 'Anglo-Scandinavian sculpture in Yorkshire', *Viking York and the North* (ed. R. A. Hall) (Council for British Archaeological Research Report 27), London 1978, 11–20.

143–4 J. T. Lang, 'Some late pre-Conquest crosses in Ryedale, Yorkshire; a reappraisal', *The Journal of the British Archaeological Association*, 1973, 16–25.

145 C. D. Morris, 'Pre-Conquest sculpture of the Tees Valley', *Medieval Archaeology* xx (1976), 140–46.

145–6 D. M. Wilson, 'Two plates from an Anglo-Saxon casket', *The Antiquaries Journal* xxxvi (1956), 31–9.

146 *Idem*, 'The King's School, Canterbury, disc brooch', *Medieval Archaeology* iv (1960), 16–28.

146 *Victoria County History, Wiltshire*, ii (1955).

146 C. A. Ralegh Radford, 'The church of St Alkmund, Derby', *Derbyshire Archaeological Journal* xcvi (1976), 26–61.

147 D. M. Wilson, 'Manx memorial stones of the Viking Age', *Saga Book* xviii (1970–71), 1–18.

149 H. Schmidt, 'The Trelleborg house reconsidered', *Medieval Archaeology* xvii (1973), 52–77.

149–50 K. Berg, 'The Gosforth Cross', *Journal of the Warburg and Courtauld Institutes* xxi (1958), 27–43.

149–50 J. T. Lang, 'Sigurd and Weland in pre-Conquest carving from northern England', *The Yorkshire Archaeological Journal* xlviii (1976), 83–94.

152ff. D. Parsons (ed.), *Tenth-century studies*, London 1975.

154–5 C. F. Battiscombe (ed.), *The relics of St Cuthbert*, Oxford 1956.

155–7 F. Wormald, 'The "Winchester School" before St Æthelwold', *England before the Conquest* (ed. P. Clemoes and K. Hughes), Cambridge 1971, 305–14.

160 D. A. Hinton, S. Keene, K. E. Qualmann, 'The Winchester Reliquary', *Medieval Archaeology* xxv (1981), 45–77.

160–72 F. Wormald, *The Benedictional of St Ethelwold*, London 1959.

179–90 F. Wormald, *English drawings of the tenth and eleventh century*, London 1952.

180–82 I. Gollancz, *The Caedmon Manuscript*, London 1927 (a facsimile),

180 B. Raw, 'The probable derivation of most of the illustrations in Junius 11 from an illustrated Old Saxon *Genesis*', *Anglo-Saxon England* v (1976), 133–49.

180 P. J. Lucas, 'MS Junius 11 and Malmesbury', *Scriptorium* xxxiv (1980), 197–220.

187 F. Wormald, 'An English eleventh-century psalter with pictures: British Museum Cotton MS Tiberius C.VI', *The Walpole Society* xxxviii (1962), 1–13.

190 *Cathédrale Saint-Michel, Trésors d'art et d'histoire*, Brussels 1975.

193–5 P. Nelson, 'An ancient box-wood casket', *Archaeologia* lxxxvi (1937), 91–100.

195 T. A. Heslop, 'English seals from the mid ninth century to 1100', *Journal of the British Archaeological Association* cxxxiii (1980), 1–16.

195–200 R. Cramp, 'Tradition and innovation in English stone sculpture of the tenth and eleventh centuries', *Kolloquium über spätantike und frühmittelalterliche Skulptur* iii (ed. V. Milojčić), Mainz 1974, 139–48.

195–200 D. Tweddle, 'Anglo-Saxon sculpture in south-east England before *c*.950', *Studies in medieval sculpture* (ed. F. H. Thompson), London 1983, 18–40.

195 J. West, 'A carved slab fragment from St Oswald's Priory, Gloucester', ibid., 41–53.

198–200 M. Biddle, 'Excavations at Winchester 1966: Fifth interim report', *The Antiquaries Journal* xlvii (1967), 251–79.

200 R. Cramp, 'The pre-Conquest sculptural tradition in Durham', *Medieval art and architecture at Durham Cathedral* (British Archaeological Association), 1980, 1–10.

200 E. Coatsworth, 'The four cross-heads from the chapter-house, Durham', *Anglo-Saxon and Viking Age sculpture* (ed. J. Lang) (British Archeological Reports, 49), 1978, 85–96.

200–210 S. Horn Fuglesang, *Some aspects of the Ringerike style*, Odense 1980.

209 D. M. Wilson, 'Men de ligger i London', *Skalk*, 1974 no. 5, 3–8.

209 F. Wormald, 'Decorated initials in English MSS from A.D. 900 to 1100', *Archaeologia* xci (1945), 107–35.

210–11 C. R. Dodwell, *The Canterbury School of illumination 1066–1200*, Cambridge 1954.

210–11 F. Stenton (ed.), *The Bayeux Tapestry*, London 1957.

211 G. Zarnecki, '1066 and architectural sculpture', *Proceedings of the British Academy* lii (1966), 87–104.

211 Idem, 'The Winchester acanthus in Romanesque sculpture', *Wallraf-Richartz-Jahrbuch* xvii (1955), 211–15.

Photographic acknowledgments

A.C.L. – Brussels: 165, 166, 240; Photo Mildred Budny: 113, 155, 206; The Master and Fellows of Corpus Christi College, Cambridge: 15, 192, 193, 203; By permission of the Syndics of Cambridge University Library: 100, 276; The Cleveland Museum of Art, Purchase from the J. H. Wade Fund: 243, 244, 245, 246; The Conway Library, Courtauld Institute of Art, London: 43, 65, 66, 67, 68, 69, 71, 72, 73, 85, 86, 87, 88, 89, 91, 92, 201; Museums and Art Gallery, Derby: 180, 181; National Museum of Ireland, Dublin: 150, 151; Royal Irish Academy, Dublin (photo The Green Studio Ltd): 21; The Board of Trinity College, Dublin (photo The Green Studio Ltd): 12, 13, 22, 24, 25, 147, 148; The Dean and Chapter of Durham Cathedral: 10, 11, 18, 26, 27, 31, 40, 42, 44, 53, 205, 207; Department of Archaeology, University of Durham (photo Tom Middlemas): 45, 46, 47, 48, 49, 50, 74, 76, 78, 79, 127, 128, 131 (photo James Lang), 141, 169, 175, 176, 177 (photo Alan Wiper), 183, 187, 188, 189, 252 (photo Rosemary Cramp), 259, 260; National Museum of Antiquities of Scotland, Edinburgh: 139, 140, 149; Biblioteca Medicea Laurenziana, Florence (photo Guido Sansoni): 39; Augustinermuseum, Freiburg: 156, Giraudon, avec autorisation speciale de la Ville de Bayeux: 277; James Lang: 168; State Public Library, Leningrad: 54, 55; By permission of the Dean and Chapter of Lichfield Cathedral: 32, 98 (photo Victoria and Albert Museum, London), 99 (photo Conway Library, Courtauld Institute of Art, London); Merseyside County Museums, Liverpool: 242; The British Library, London: 29, 30, 38, 103, 111, 112, 114, 216, 218, 219, 220, 221, 222, 223, 230, 231, 232, 234, 235, 236, 261, 263, 264; Reproduced by courtesy of the Trustees of the British Museum, London: 1, 2, 3, 4, 5, 6, 7, 8, 9, 16, 17, 33, 34, 35, 36, 37, 51, 62, 77,

Index